A NEWCOMER'S GUIDE TO THE AFTERLIFE

A NEWCOMER'S GUIDE TO THE

AFTERLIFE

On the Other Side known commonly as *"The Little Book"*

DANIEL QUINN

TOM WHALEN

Illustrations by Greg Boyd

BANTAM BOOKS
New York   Toronto   London   Sydney   Auckland

A NEWCOMER'S GUIDE TO THE AFTERLIFE
A Bantam Book / August 1997

BOOK DESIGN BY GLEN M. EDELSTEIN

PHOTO COLLAGES BY GREG BOYD

Library of Congress Cataloging-in-Publication Data

Quinn, Daniel.
A newcomer's guide to the afterlife: on the other side known commonly as
The little book/Daniel Quinn, Tom Whalen.
p.   cm.
Includes bibliographical references and index.
ISBN 0-553-09670-2
I. Near-death experiences—Religious aspects—Humor.   2. Future life—Humor.
I. Whalen, Tom.   II. Title.
PS 3567.U338N49   1997
818'.5402—DC20   94-24558
CIP

Published simultaneously in the United States and Canada

Bantam Books are published by Bantam Books, a division of Bantam Doubleday Dell Publishing
Group, Inc. Its trademark, consisting of the words "Bantam Books" and the portrayal of a rooster,
is Registered in U.S. Patent and Trademark Office and in other countries. Marca Registrada.
Bantam Books, 1540 Broadway, New York, New York 10036.

PRINTED IN THE UNITED STATES OF AMERICA

BVG   10 9 8 7 6 5 4 3 2 1

CONTENTS

LIST OF ILLUSTRATIONS

INTRODUCTION

I HAVE TO BEGIN THIS INTRODUCTION WITH A confession: that it was originally my intention to offer a lie to explain how this book came into being.

I planned to offer this lie in an introduction supposedly written by the publishers (whoever they might prove to be), explaining that the manuscript for the book had come to them from an unknown, unagented author we'll call Jones. In his cover letter, Jones explained that, as a result of an accident that had occurred some months before, he had spent six minutes clinically dead. During this Near-Death Experience (NDE), Jones wandered in a muddled state through an unfamiliar urban landscape until he stopped a stranger and asked where he was. This stranger, recognizing the cause of Jones's bewilderment, handed him a small book, saying that Jones was welcome to keep it. Jones replied that it wouldn't be necessary for him to keep it because he had an eidetic memory; by merely glancing at the pages, he would be able to carry away the entire book, every last jot and tittle of it, unread, in his memory. He quickly paged through the book, returned it to its owner, and moments later was restored to life in a hospital emergency room. Several months passed before Jones remembered that he had the text of an unknown book lying in his head; "reading" it in memory, he realized that he had brought back from his NDE nothing less than a guidebook written for new arrivals to the Afterlife, which he duly transcribed for earthly publication.

It was, I thought, a clever invention—and perhaps not strictly speaking a lie at all, since I didn't actually expect or intend anyone to be deceived by it.

And now for the truth, which, as usual, is not nearly as tidy as the invention.

I'd been working for almost a year on *Providence*, an autobiographical work tracing the origins of *Ishmael*, the book for which I am best known. It was being written in the form of a dialogue between myself and a stranger, who, according to the framing story of the book, invades my house one night and demands answers to certain questions. Then one night a few months ago, I had a dream that was almost identical to this framing story. Trudging half-asleep (in my dream) from bathroom to bedroom in the middle of the night, I was startled to see someone sitting on a sofa in the living room—startled but not frightened, because this was plainly not a burglar or a mad slasher come to do us in. Drawing nearer and turning up the lights, I saw, in fact, that it was not a stranger at all, though it was certainly a strange person to find visiting my house in the middle of the night. It was Delores Elaine Pierce, head of the post office where I maintained a box for mail from readers of *Ishmael*. This was in fact a U.S. Post Office Contract Station, rather than a fully fledged post office, and the whole operation could probably have fit into my living room without squeezing. In terms of personnel, Delores was it; she sorted the mail, filled the boxes, and manned the window. She was an attractive, cheerful, and personable woman in her forties, and we were on a first-name basis almost from the first day of our acquaintance.

So as to be able to include the number of the postal box in my book, I'd had to rent it nearly a year before the book actually came out, and by the time the first piece of mail arrived, my wife and I had moved to the other side of the city. I explained the situation to Delores, who said it would be no trouble for her to forward the mail to our new location. However, it soon became obvious to me that it *was* trouble, and I told her to let the mail accumulate and I'd collect it every Saturday. As well as letters, a number of interesting parcels arrived, including, among other things, a framed, life-size photographic portrait of a gorilla, and I saw no reason not to let Delores know what was going on. In fact, I gave her a copy of the book so she could see for herself how the box was being used. She enjoyed this contact with "a famous author" and confided that she too harbored an ambition to "write a book someday."

We became quite friendly, and I missed her whenever she took a vacation and a stranger appeared in her place at the window.

Then, as I say, one night she appeared in my living room, in a dream. I told her how surprised I was to see her there.

"I have some mail for you," she said, handing me a bulky envelope.

"You shouldn't have bothered," I told her. "I'll be by on Saturday, as usual."

"I know, but I thought this might be urgent."

The envelope contained a small, perfectly blank paperbound book about four inches by five and three-quarters of an inch thick. I frowned in puzzlement, but Delores seemed very impressed by it. "Now *that's* the book you should be working on," she said. I pointed out that it wasn't much of a book, since the pages were blank, but she had a good explanation for that: "The pages are blank because you haven't filled them up yet."

"What do you think I should fill them with?"

To my total astonishment, she said: "I think you should write a guidebook for the dead."

I stared at her dumbfounded for a moment, then asked why on earth I should do that.

"Because, when people arrive in the Afterlife, they're very confused at first. They don't know where they are or what's going on."

"I'm sure that's true," I said, "but how do I come into it? I don't know anything about the Afterlife."

"I can help you with that part," Delores replied. "You remember I once told you I wanted to write a book of my own?"

I said I did.

"Well, this is it."

I stared at her in disbelief. "You want to write a guide to the Afterlife?"

"That's right."

"Then why do you need me? You can write it yourself."

"Oh, you know what it's like down at the station. I never have any time."

"Well, it's an intriguing idea," I had to admit. "But if you don't have time to write it yourself, I don't see how you're going to have time to help *me* write it."

"You can keep that," she said, nodding at the book.

I looked down and saw that the pages of the book were no longer blank; I had the impression that Delores had somehow "downloaded" her thoughts directly onto the paper. What I saw fascinated me, and Delores ceased to be the focal point of the dream. I spent the rest of the night reading in that nightmarish way of dreams, in which everything seems to make brilliant sense for a moment and then collapses into chaos and gibberish.

When I woke in the morning, I realized I had "dreamed up" a terrific idea for a book. An immediate difficulty came to mind: If this was supposed to be the guidebook that the dead receive on arrival in the Afterlife, how would it come to be published on earth? A little thought gave me an answer to that: If someone with an eidetic memory were to have an NDE lasting long enough for him to get a copy of the guidebook and scan it, then he would return to life with the complete text in his head and would only have to type it out to produce a publishable manuscript. For anyone who accepts the possibility of having an NDE, there's nothing inherently incredible in this premise; after all, no experience of *anything* occurs unless there's a memory of it, and if one is capable of having a memory of an NDE, then why not an *eidetic* memory of it?

While I had it in mind, I sat down and wrote the introduction described above. That done, I was ready to make a start on the book itself.

I found that my dream had left me with a number of surprisingly strong impressions, chief among them that of the Afterlife author who had created the guidebook (and whose voice I would be adopting in the text); he was a tad stuffy, a tad pedantic, and perhaps a tad more formal than modern readers are used to, though all this seemed suitable to a man who had spent his lifetime, as I imagined it, during the first half of the nineteenth century. I even had a name for this gentleman—James Catnach—who had evidently been producing the guidebook for a long time, since this was the forty-ninth edition. (Though the book is undated, internal evidence places it clearly in the 1990s.)

The "reading" I'd done in my dream hadn't given me a text, but it had given me all the information I needed to *produce* a text, or so it seemed to me at the outset. I'd told Delores that I didn't know anything about the Afterlife, but I now seemed to know *everything*. I felt prepared to answer any question a newcomer might ask and thought it would make good sense to open the book with a fairly lengthy Q & A section, "Basic Questions Answered." This kept me happily busy for several days.

As I worked, however, I began to feel uneasy about certain

"dark" portions of the book. I call them dark because I knew they were there—but only by the shadows they cast. I thought I knew why they were dark; they were texts imported from other sources, and I had the impression that they were very alien to Catnach's reasonable tone and commonsense approach to conditions in the Afterlife. Catnach felt obliged to include these alien texts in his book (perhaps for the very reason that they *were* alien), but they represented irrational and unruly intrusions into the tidy presentation he wanted to make. Perhaps he didn't really want to see them in his book at all, and for that reason I hadn't been able to see them clearly myself. Although they troubled me, I decided to worry about them later. After all, I had plenty of other material to keep me busy—or so I imagined. In fact, one morning I powered up my word processor, brought up the text from the hard disk, and discovered I didn't have a word to add to what was already there.

I was startled and puzzled. I'd had no hint that I was on the verge of running out of material, and in an odd way I knew I *hadn't* run out of material. There are computer programs that can take an image and scramble it into what looks like a featureless array of dots and scrawls. To the straightforward glance, there is utterly nothing to be seen in this array, but if you can manage to gaze at it with an unfocused stare, your brain will obligingly *unscramble* the image, which will spring forth from the surface of the printed sheet with astonishing depth. For as long as you maintain this stare, you can move your eyes from place to place in the picture and discover details that seem almost uncanny in their clarity, but close one eye and the image vanishes instantly and completely. You know as a certainty that the image is there, but not a trace of it can be discovered without resuming that un-focused stare. It was that way with me and the material of Catnach's book. I knew it was there, but I'd somehow lost the knack of accessing it.

Another person might have decided to relax and wait for the knack to return, but that's not my way. I struggled and strove for the next two days without making any progress at all. The "Other Side" was blocked from sight . . . at least from waking sight.

On the second night, however, I visited the Afterlife in my dreams.

I knew where I was without being told, as one does in dreams. It was, as I'd already written, quite an ordinary sort of place—a desert, though it lacked all the negative qualities associated with earthly deserts. It wasn't hot or bleak or sandy, it was just empty.

I was walking in a dry river bed toward a revelation that would, I felt, solve all my problems. I was going to be shown something that would sweep away all my difficulties. In fact, I could see it already, on the horizon, or in the air just above the horizon, a kind of vortex of turbulence with an undulant black thread at its center. As I approached it, I realized that the river bed was not exactly empty; air and light and power were being powerfully drawn (as I was) toward the object hovering at the horizon.

Before long, the land in front of me fell away into an enor-mous valley hundreds of miles wide, and the river bed plunged into it and then divided and subdivided countlessly to form a vast, exquisite delta reaching out into an ocean not of water but of seething energy, which flowed inexhaustibly upward into that vortex of turbulence, which now (from my vantage point) stood about forty-five degrees above the horizon.

At the center of the vortex, I knew as a certainty, swam Leviathan. This was the "black thread" I'd seen from a distance. Only in dreams can one witness such awesome events as the swimming of Leviathan. I stood, enchanted, as this gleaming beast poured gracefully and with infinite slowness through the turbulence of which it was the center. It was, I soon understood, the *cause* of the turbulence. More, the turbulence was the result of the flow of matter and energy *into* Leviathan from all sides— from the sky above, from the "ocean," from the river, and even from the land, which I could see clearly being drawn upward like a tenuous mist. This was the "source"; this was the fountainhead of the Afterlife, perhaps of the cosmos itself. All matter and energy flowed up into Leviathan and was endlessly renewed within it. I watched, fascinated, enthralled, and would have been content to watch forever. . . .

You might expect I would have awakened the next morning disappointed that I hadn't been "shown something that would sweep away all my difficulties," but this wasn't the case. I awoke knowing exactly what I needed. I needed a collaborator, and what's more I knew who the collaborator should be: Tom Whalen of New Orleans, a writer I'd never met in person or even spoken to on the phone but whose work had a clear resonance with my own. (There was a time, later on, when I thought that my dream had "suggested" him to me: *Leviathan = Whale = Whalen* and *Delta = Mississippi Delta = New Orleans.* Now I'm inclined to think it was the other way around.) We'd been in correspondence for about three years, trading clips of our stories, but had never discussed the possibility of collaborating on anything. I lost no time in writing to explain what I was working on and what I had in mind.

His reply astonished me: He had *already written extensively on the Afterlife*—and he enclosed an amount of material equal to all that I had produced so far! I say that I was astonished, but I should add that I was not dumbfounded or anything remotely like it. After all, I'd thought of Tom precisely because I'd noticed a resonance between his work and mine; if I was writing on the Afterlife, why should I be amazed that he was doing the same? It was only later on, as they began to accumulate, that the coincidences began to seem uncanny.

The correspondences between Tom's vision of the Afterlife and mine were remarkable. For example, both assumed the existence of a small, popular guidebook; in his material, it was referred to as *The Little Book*, and as soon as I saw it I became convinced (wishful thinking, perhaps) that this was the title of the book I'd seen in my dream. Both of us saw the Afterlife as "ordinary" and "unheavenly." Undoubtedly the most important correspondence occurred in the matter of the "peopling" of the Afterlife. In my dream "reading" of Catnach's guidebook, I had seen that three distinct types of shades existed on the Other Side. One type, the most prominent, was made up of people who were recognizably "us." These, in Tom's *Little Book*, were identified as *Regulars*. The two other types, of which I had been unable to form a clear picture, were named by Tom *Husks* and *Adepts*. Although I'd been unable to form a clear picture of them until then, I recognized them at once from his descriptions. (Again, perhaps "wishful thinking.") More important, *I knew who they were*—and Tom did not. Tom could see that they existed and could describe them but was unable to identify them, was unable to explain what they were doing in the Afterlife. In this instance and many others, each of us possessed a key piece of data that the other lacked.

We were, in addition, complementary on a broader level. As I've said, I was aware of portions of the book that were "dark" to me, because they were texts that Catnach had imported from "alien" sources. These texts, inaccessible to me, were already in Tom Whalen's files. Where he'd "seen" them, I don't know; I've never asked and don't plan to ask.

I described earlier the coded images that can only be decoded by an unfocused stare. I should have added that they can only be decoded by a *binocular* stare. With Tom at work, I had, in effect, attained binocular vision. The "code" had been broken, and I was now once again able to access the text of Catnach's little book.

Work went smoothly for another two weeks.

By that time I was becoming a little irked by Delores's absence from the post office. I'm a fusspot in this regard and like to see people where I'm used to seeing them. So, when I arrived to pick up my mail on Saturday, I confronted the young woman who was filling in for Delores during her vacation.

"When is Delores going to be back?" I demanded to know.

She gazed at me solemnly and said: "Delores is dead."

I gawked at her, thunderstruck.

"She was killed in an auto accident in Tallahassee, right at the beginning of her vacation. Her husband brought in this clipping from the newspaper."

Taped to the wall right beside me was a two-inch obituary, which included the surprising fact that Delores, whom I'd taken to be in her late forties, had been sixty-seven at the time of her death. I retreated in a funk.

I couldn't recall the exact date on which Delores had visited my dreams to urge me to write a guide for newcomers to the Afterlife and to offer me her help with it. It was certainly after the beginning of her vacation, since I remembered thinking I would tell her about the dream when she returned.

I like to think that I'm a rational and nonsuperstitious person, but I'm afraid I was initially inclined to be profoundly unnerved by this eerie coincidence. Put nakedly, the question was this: Had I received in my dream an actual, first-hand account of what it's like to arrive in the Afterlife (people are "very confused at first," Delores had told me)? I was at first unable to answer that question the way I wanted to answer it, which was with a confident *No! Don't be ridiculous!*

Later that same day I received a new batch of material from Tom Whalen, including a new entry for the Q & A section. The question Tom sent was: "What is the smoke I see on the horizon? Are those whales? Is that an ocean?" I hadn't told Tom about my dream of the "Leviathan," and therefore hadn't shared with him my perception that it was "the fountainhead of the Afterlife."

At this point, I'm ashamed to say, I lost my nerve. I immediately sat down and wrote Tom a letter suggesting that it might be best to shut down our collaboration, citing minor discrepancies between "his version" and "my version" and offering the feeble opinion that I might not be sufficiently "great-souled" for such an enterprise (whatever *that* might mean). Luckily for us both (and for the book), he wrote back immediately to reassure me that the discrepancies I'd noted were of slight importance (as was the case, of course) and should be handled in whatever way I thought best.

For the time being, however, I wanted nothing more to do with the project. Besides, I had to get back to work on *Providence*, which I had promised myself would be finished in the spring of 1993.

After a few weeks of work, I fulfilled that promise.

In the interval I visited Delores's post office every Saturday and reexamined the obituary taped to the wall beside the window. (It was still taped there at this writing.) Gradually I began to frame a new hypothesis, based on the fact that this obituary had been taped to the wall for *at least* two weeks before my attention was drawn to it. Perhaps, this hypothesis suggested, it was there even before I had my dream about Delores. If so, my eye had certainly fallen upon it. Although I had utterly no *conscious* awareness that Delores was dead, is it possible that I had *unconsciously* registered the fact of her death and then worked this into a dream about her? It's not inconceivable that, while I was digging mail out of my box, someone a few feet away at the window was saying, "I can't believe it! Delores is *dead*?" I certainly heard no such thing . . . but then I wasn't *listening* for such a thing; my mind was on my mail. Even so, those syllables, if uttered, could conceivably have entered my subconscious, where they might have been processed for presentation to me as a dream. Implausible as this sounds, it's certainly *more* plausible than receiving a visit from a ghost ready to help me write a book on the Afterlife.

In any case, by the time I was ready to resume work on *The Little Book* I had regained my nerve. One thing was certain, however: The book needed a very different sort of introduction from the one I had originally planned.

This is it.

Daniel Quinn
June, 1993

THE
LITTLE
BOOK

A Newcomer's Guide to the Afterlife

49th Edition

JAMES CATNACH

CHAPTER 1

BASIC
QUESTIONS
ANSWERED

Q. **What am I doing here? I feel totally disoriented and helpless.**

A. This is normal for the newly dead and will pass.
    Your circumstances have changed as drastically as it is
    possible for circumstances to change. Every single one
    of us felt this way initially. Every single one of us
    eventually learned the ropes and regained our sense of
    balance and self-possession. *The Little Book* is designed
    to serve as a ready first aid to this objective.

Q. What's wrong with my legs? It's as though they
were made of rubber.

A. You have what is popularly known as the staggers,
which we all have when we arrive in the Afterlife.
You'll be back to normal in a few days.

Q. Exactly where am I?

A. In life, it seemed to you that you inhabited a universe
of stars, galaxies, and so on, and you located yourself
as an individual on the planet Earth, on one of its
continents or islands, perhaps in one of its cities. In
your stay in that universe, this seemed "normal." A
quick look round will convince you that you no longer
inhabit that universe. It's said that we inhabit "another
dimension" or "a parallel universe," but these phrases
have no precise meaning. Basically, you're *somewhere else,*
and this somewhere else will soon seem completely
normal to you.

Q. But everything already *looks* completely normal.

A. Our environment is locally psycho-reactive, which is
to say that it responds to our individual expectations
in ways that are not explainable in ordinary causal
terms. If you are, let us say, an American urbanite of
the 1990s, your surroundings will almost certainly
look and function like a sort of idealized American

4

city of that era. If, on the other hand, you are a Kayapo Indian of the 1990s, your surroundings will look and function like a rain forest in the interior of Brazil.

Q. Is this heaven then?

A. Some believe so. Some argue that it cannot be, since no divine presence makes itself felt. Some believe it to be a purgatory from which some or all of us will eventually be delivered. Even in the Afterlife, questions remain.

Q. Why do people call this place Detroit [Nepal, Havana, Beijing, Hong Kong, Sheffield, Nebraska]? It isn't at all the way I remember it.

A. Place names in the Afterlife are not subject to any objective standard. Several large French cities are named Paris, and they are not all in the same general area (not, in other words, all in "France"). Shades in your area (or at least some of them) have adopted the habit of calling it Detroit (or whatever). It doesn't mean much of anything. Humor them—or call it whatever you please (maybe you'll start a new trend).

Q. Are maps available?

A. Yes, and they are delightful to look upon. Maps as small as your thumb, maps as large as the landscape.

Minutely detailed maps with names of places you've never been. Glorious maps, filigreed, flagged, annotated, and totally impractical.

Q. Why is it always overcast? Doesn't the sun ever shine?

A. It isn't "overcast," and there is no sun to shine. The light (and the alternation of "day" and "night") is assumed to be our environment's response to our expectations of it. Finicky speakers say that we *experience* light (and the rest of the Afterlife), not that light (or anything else in the Afterlife) *exists*. If you would prefer to pass your time entirely in the "day," you will want to search out one of the so-called Northern Cities, where "the sun shines twenty-four hours a day."

Q. What is my body made of?

A. The nature of matter in this continuum (including the matter in your body) is as mysterious as the nature of matter in the continuum we knew when alive. Clearly our bodies are not as "substantial" as in life— not as heavy or impermeable.

Q. I thought memory was a brain function, pure and simple. How can I have memories if I don't have a brain?

A. You clearly *do* have a brain, just as you clearly have arms, legs, eyes, nose, hair, and so on. All the organs are there, though their function may or may not be.

Q. **I don't have any feeling of hunger, but I've seen people eating. Will I get hungry later?**

A. Food is not a necessity in the Afterlife. "Eating" (it has to be enclosed in quotation marks) is an experience quite unlike the one you knew in life. Try it, and spare me the necessity of describing something you will inevitably experience for yourself.

Q. **What about sleep? Do people sleep here?**

A. People rest, doze, tune out, power down, and, yes, sleep (though neurologists insist that none of these states actually correspond to what the living call sleep). Some find they have no need of it, some spend as much time at it as they can. It continues to provide a handy means of ending a tiresome visit: "I have to go home and sleep now, thank you. *Auf Wiedersehen!*"

Q. **What's the proper way to talk about things here? Do you call people ghosts or spirits or what?**

A. You may call people people. People are called ghosts or shades only in a semi-jocular or casual way, except when referring to their former status, as in, "Today I met the shade of my second cousin Alf." (Most people, however, would simply say, "Today I met my second cousin Alf.") You will seldom hear people refer to us as spirits. Most people think of spirits as bodiless beings (which we are clearly not).

Q. **Do people refer to themselves as dead?**

A. We often refer to ourselves collectively as "the dead" but as individuals seldom think of ourselves as such, since we are manifestly alive (though in a somewhat attenuated form). We say, "I live two streets over," "This is not a bad life we have here," "I live for my work," "I prefer to live alone," and so on.

Q. **I worry that, being a newcomer, I may inadvertently violate some custom or give offense to someone. Are there guides to etiquette and good manners?**

A. Such guides exist, though they were more in evidence in the seventeenth, eighteenth, and nineteenth centuries. In general, the good manners you practiced in life will serve perfectly well here. Special customs do not seem to arise among the dead; if you think about it, you'll see that the conditions and occasions that fostered the development of customs in life are largely absent here.

Q. I heard someone talk about "losing his head." What
does this mean?

A. Losing your head is a sort of jocular euphemism for
dying; the reference is of course to decapitation. When
in a few days or weeks you have recovered from the
shock of "losing your head," it will be said that you
"have your head on"—in other words, are once again
whole.

Q. An awful lot of people I see in the street look and
act like lunatics. Many of them tell me they don't
know who they are. What's the story here?

A. To answer briefly: Standards of normalcy are
somewhat different in the Afterlife. For more on this,
see Chapter Three, "Neighbors in the Afterlife."

Q. But I've heard people talk about a Bedlam here in
the Afterlife as if it were a real lunatic asylum. Is
there such a place, or is this just a rumor?

A. People who in life inhabited Bucharest or Baltimore
"wake up" in the Afterlife in a place that seems to
them very like Bucharest or Baltimore. The same is
true of people who in life inhabited London's Bethlem
Hospital, the madhouse known popularly as Bedlam.
Thus Bedlam is as "real" as any other place in the
Afterlife; its inhabitants tend to be lunatics, just as the

inhabitants of "Dublin" tend to be Irish. Since their environment is psycho-reactive in exactly the same way ours is, Bedlam is veritably a bedlam, operating under its own chaotic and delusional laws.

Q. Where should I go? Should I "check in" someplace?

A. No, there is no special procedure or induction for newcomers.

Q. But where am I supposed to stay?

A. You will eventually want to find a space of your own, of course, but your present-felt need for shelter is more psychological than physical. I mean that you're not in any *danger* (as you might well be in the same circumstances in life). You don't in fact need protection from either the elements or the people around you.

Q. Can I just go where I please then?

A. For the most part, yes. No one "owns" the Afterlife or any part of it. On the other hand, people tend to make the space around them their own, and this is something you will want to respect. For more on this subject, see Chapter Three.

Q. How do I get around? Is there mass transit? Cabs? Bicycles?

A. Mostly by means of bipedal locomotion. Look around you and you'll see few if any vehicles. A bicycle, perhaps, yes, but no cars, or if cars, then doubtless Phantasms, invariably blue in color, which vanish when approached. Carts, wheelbarrows, and rickshaws are seen, but their function is probably ornamental since one seldom sees them in use. For the most part, we walk. And walk and walk. "Where are you going?" "Down the road." No one says "up" the road. We walk, sometimes fast, sometimes slow, occasionally we run. In the streets, in the so-called malls, on the road. We walk and walk. But as often, simply stand. Stand and stare, or not stare.

Q. Will the clothes I have on eventually wear out?

A. Yes, but that's not a cause for worry. Stores (in the sense of "accumulations of goods") are found everywhere in the Afterlife, and you are at liberty to take what you want from them. To be honest, you may never find the clothes you like when you're looking for them. For example, you may want to wear dungarees but can only find, in your size, an evening gown, albeit a quite lovely one. In the end, what you wear simply doesn't matter; soon enough you'll lose your self-consciousness about such things.

Q. If I had an addiction to, say, coffee, sweets, cigarettes, illegal substances of a variety of sorts, will my addiction still be with me, and if so, how will I satisfy my need?

A. Desires come and go. Desires fade. One hypothesis, avidly promoted by Professors Burroughs, Bradley, and Lee, is that the Afterlife is in itself a kind of addiction, an hallucinatory high with no side effects. Appealing as this hypothesis is to some (and you're welcome to it if you wish), it bears little relationship to the facts.

Q. You mentioned "professors." Are there universities in the Afterlife?

A. No degree-offering institutions exist. Titles such as Professor or Doctor are usually carried over from one's previous existence, though you may of course call yourself whatever you please.

Q. What is the smoke I see on the horizon?[1] Are those whales? Is that an ocean?

---

[1] There is no true horizon anywhere in the Afterlife. The horizon we perceived in life as a line dividing earth from sky was a perceptual construct forced upon us by the curvature of the earth. The Afterlife gives every appearance of being a plane surface extending indefinitely in all directions. At a distance of about a hundred kilometers from any viewer, dust, moisture, and other particles in the atmosphere combine to create a more or less impenetrable haze, and objects within this haze are said to be (and are experienced as being) "on the horizon."

A. If you see the "whales," you're rare. Few people do, but enough "sightings" have occurred to warrant extensive study of the subject. No, what you see are not whales or smoke or even an ocean, though that withdrawing roar does resemble the sound of waves receding from a shore. Pozler theorizes, in a manner reminiscent of Hoyle's Steady State theory of the universe, that this is the primordial matter from which the Afterlife takes its sustenance. The most advanced hypothesis put forth to date is that what you are seeing are tachyons, particles that travel faster than light. Physicists are proposing that if they are tachyons and tachyons form the base matter of the Afterlife, then we are traveling faster than light, thus accounting for the fact that no one grows old here. Husks decay, yes, and skin falls off the bodies of some; but in general nothing truly ages.

Q. **Can death occur in the Afterlife, and if so, is there a life after Afterlife?**

A. Many of the deceased would like to believe so. See Chapter Five, "Religions of the Afterlife."

Q. **Does everyone who dies come to this place?**

A. If infants and small children arrive here as Husks, then presumably yes. The fact that you may not be able to find your great-great-grandmother doesn't prove she isn't here, somewhere; on the other hand, there is no way to prove that she *is* here, unless you find her.

Q. **My apparent age is about** *x.* **Why didn't I arrive in the Afterlife younger or older? Will I stay this age?**

A. Most people seem to feel that they arrived in the Afterlife at their peak (though many will admit that this may be a rationalization). It's true, for example, that the shades of athletes tend to be "younger" than those whose achievements depended on maturity and experience. No answer is forthcoming for those who ask why they couldn't have been translated to the Afterlife younger or older; a few years ago I was informed that this was "just the way the cookie crumbles." You will not age or grow younger.

Q. **Why am I cold?**

A. Because you are dead, and the *prana* (rosy light) that cascades through your remains, though beautiful, offers no real warmth.

Q. **Who's "in charge" here?**

A. No one is in charge. There is no civil, moral, religious, or other authority. None is needed or would serve any purpose. This is a source of disappointment to those who arrive ready to demand special treatment, lodge a complaint, or petition for "another chance" at life.

Q. **Who is this Enemy I hear people talking about?**

A. The Enemy is the bugbear, bogey, and bugaboo of simple souls in the Afterlife. The Enemy is the ogre under the bed and the monster in the closet—in short, the product of superstition and fearful imagination.

Q. **Who is the Dark Brother?**

A. The Dark Brother is an archetypal figure of fantasy, mythology, or religion, depending on your point of view. He is dark because "the light does not shine upon him"—that is, he is hidden. He is hidden (so goes the belief) in each one of us at some time or other—without our knowledge—perhaps for a moment, perhaps for a day, perhaps for a year. He is "the one we lost and that which we lost." If he were ever to be assuredly "found" and revealed, he would lead us into a new era or state of existence. The Guild of the Dark Brother is one of the oldest and largest in the Afterlife.

Q. **What does one *do* here?**

A. As in life, one exists. No occupation as such is necessary. Even though your body is unchanged in appearance, it no longer functions as a biological organism. You will never grow hungry or thirsty, never fall sick, never grow older, and (of course) never die.

Q. **But what do people do to pass the time?**

A. Guilds, clubs, and religions (discussed in detail in later chapters) absorb much time and energy. Basically, people do the same things they did in life, with the obvious exceptions.

Q. **You mean, if I always wanted to be a filmmaker, I could make a new version of *Ben-Hur*?**

A. It would be difficult—as it was in life—to make a new version of *Ben-Hur*. Since no one needs to work in order to live, you would be unable to hire laborers to build sets, for example. You might have difficulty locating or constructing suitable optical equipment. People would work on the project only if you could make it seem worth doing in and of itself. Other difficulties would arise when it came to distributing and exhibiting your film.

Q. **You mean there is no film industry.**

A. There is no industry of any type or description.

For those in search of inspiration, behold Jessie Clowthy and Ralph Guddren, who insist that, in life, they were "just ordinary folks." In the Afterlife they are everywhere loved and admired as the Mother of Clouds and the Father of Cities—vocations they invented for themselves without guidance or example. As shown in this photograph, Miss Clowthy typically caps her associate's work by emptying her "sack of clouds" to create a vast panorama of dramatic effects seldom seen in the normal course of events.

Q. **Suppose I want a hundred-room mansion with indoor and outdoor swimming pools?**

A. Build one, by all means. Build a dozen, if you like. After all, you have eternity in which to work.

Q. **Can I hire people to do things for me?**

A. Using what currency? People have no need for money in the Afterlife, but, seeing someone at work, they will often pitch in simply to pass the time or to make an acquaintance. And people often exchange work for work; the bartering of services in the Afterlife is a lively and complex activity.

Q. **On the subject of construction, isn't there a shortage of space, considering all the people who have died?**

A. The physical arrangement of this "parallel universe" is somewhat different from the one you knew in life. Earlier peoples do not share our space. Rather, they share our time, which is unlimited.

Q. **Could you expand on that a bit?**

A. If you'd like to have a conversation with Christopher Columbus, you won't find him a few thousand miles away. You will find him five hundred *years* away.

Traveling in time is easily learned but does not lend itself to explanation by way of the written word. It's like riding a bicycle, you learn it by doing it.

Q. **Can I travel into the future?**

A. Alas, no. Travel into the past is like diving. To travel back a few years is very easy, like dipping your head below the surface of the water. To travel back a few decades is like swimming a few feet below the surface. The farther back you go in time, the deeper (and more strenuous) the dive. But after each dive, you can only return to the surface, which is to say to your present. The time traveler can no more leap up out of the present into the future than a swimmer can leap up out of the water into the air.

Q. **What special powers do the dead have?**

A. The dead have no powers that would seem special to the living. They are relatively feeble, much as the classical writers of Greece and Rome imagined them to be.

Q. **Isn't the ability to travel into the past a special power?**

A. To describe it as travel into the past is to speak somewhat loosely. We merely travel into regions inhabited by those who have died before us. We can have a chat with William the Conqueror, but that doesn't enable us to watch the Battle of Hastings (much less influence its outcome). Since there is nothing we can "do" with this power, it hardly seems to qualify as one.

Q. **Does the arrow of time in the Afterlife travel at the same pace and in the same direction as in life?**

A. It gives every appearance of doing so. In fact, we "set our clocks" by the arrival of newcomers. Except for our own awareness of the passage of time, the Afterlife provides no objective basis for time-keeping—no rising and setting sun, no seasonal cycles, no radioactive decay. If a newcomer reports that he died on Christmas Eve, we can confidently expect a newcomer will soon arrive reporting that he died on Christmas day. And, by the way, in casual conversation, it is considered rather stuffy to continually make a point of the fact that our units of time are based only on perception. We say, "I'll meet you in an hour," "I'm leaving next week," and "I may be gone for a year," and everyone understands that these statements are approximations. A few obsessive people own watches or clocks, but most consider it utterly superfluous to keep careful track of time in eternity.

Q. What about communication with the living?

A. As in life, this is a disputed matter. Some claim to have achieved it; most believe that what is achieved is merely self-delusion. See also "Mediums" in the section "Greeters and Other Dubious Friends," in Chapter Three.

Q. How can I get in touch with friends and relatives who have passed on ahead of me?

A. Check with Central Registry, a service that has been operant since the middle of the eighteenth century.[2] There is no guarantee that any given person can be located by this means, since no one is required to register. In the Afterlife, no one is required to do anything whatever.

Q. You mean, no one knows I'm here?

A. That's right. There is no Celestial Record Book with your name in it. As far as is known, no angelic scribe was on hand at your death to expunge your name from the Book of Life.

---

[2] It should be noted that any Central Registry is central only in a local sense. There is no Central Registry for the whole of the Afterlife, nor is such a thing thinkably possible. Every Central Registry collaborates with hundreds of others to pool names and locations of the dead; the work, for the most part carried on by people looking for their own friends and relatives, is ever-increasing and obviously never-ending. Volunteers are always welcome.

Q. Suppose the person I want to find isn't registered? What do I do in that case?

A. In that case you start looking. The Afterlife is infinite in extent, but "small-world" coincidences happen all the time, just as in life. If you'd rather not undertake the search personally, you can always ask round for a reliable "Finder" (see Chapter Three).

Q. Speaking of angelic scribes, is there anything like that going on? Choirs of angels? Heavenly voices?

A. No, nothing. Nonetheless, many earthly religious practices still flourish, as do many Afterlife religions as well.

Q. What do you mean by "Afterlife" religions?

A. I mean religions that have no counterpart or antecedent among the living: religions that developed entirely among the deceased. They are discussed at length in Chapter Five.

Q. Are there animals here?

A. Yes, there are animals in the Afterlife. You will encounter dogs, cats, mice, rats, birds, snakes, frogs, and insects on roads, in houses, alleys, forests, fields;

and turtles, fish, snakes and frogs in ponds, lakes, rivers and seas.

Q. Are they more abundant than they were on earth?

A. No.

Q. Are they real?

A. Studies of animal physiology indicate that they are as "real" as you or I. The question of whether or not something is "real" will frequently arise during your first hours in the Afterlife, but soon you will realize that it yields little to doubt what you see. The world is what it is: elusive and illusive, deceptive and complex. Quain, in *The Metaphysics of Physics*, says that whatever can be imagined as not existing exists. Some newcomers find solace in this notion.

Q. Pets?

A. No. Sorry. No bonding occurs between human and animal forms in the Afterlife. Should you encounter a former pet (a highly unlikely occurrence), your pet will not rush up to you and joyfully leap about your legs. And should you excitedly rush to your former pet, the latter will turn quickly away as if embarrassed by the spectacle.

Q. Are there zoos?

A. Yes, and they are excellent.

Q. What is the difference between the soul of a human
being and that of an animal, if they have one?

A. If by "soul" you mean a spiritual entity that exists
past the body's so-called natural life, an entity that is
imbued with a "divine grace" granted by an
anthropomorphic deity for reasons only "He" can
know, then we would suggest you rethink your terms.
If on the other hand by "soul" you mean the "trace"
that has crossed over, then we can refer you to
Thrale's studies of animal and human "traces" in
which, to take one example, he found no difference
between the subatomic etheric doubles of capybaras
and their human predators along the Amazon.

Q. Are the animals here happy?

A. They do not appear sad.

Q. What about friendships, relationships, and so on?

A. As in life, have them or not, as you please.

In the Afterlife, zoological gardens often find uses that would be unimaginable among the living. Here the La Brea Memorial Wild Animal Monument provides an exotic backdrop for a recent gala of *Classe Première,* a club open only to luxury class passengers who perished in the *Titanic* marine disaster of 1912.

Q. **Romance?**

A. Certainly, why not?

Q. **Marriage?**

A. Pointless.

Q. **Sex?**

A. Believe it or not, opinions vary. Some say,
   "Absolutely yes, it's better than ever," others
   "Absolutely no, it's just a phantom activity, like
   'eating.'" On the whole, it's safe to say that sex is not
   remotely a "drive" amongst the dead.

"Wedding Procession at the Village Hall," by Robert ("Paco") Culhane. Although matrimony is a meaningless and unsanctioned institution in the Afterlife, ceremonies like this one still take place from time to time among the nostalgically inclined.

CHAPTER 2
A FEW DO'S AND DON'TS OF THE AFTERLIFE

DO MAKE A NOTE OF YOUR NAME AND KEEP IT WITH you—not because it will ever be required of you but for exactly the opposite reason, because it will *never* be required of you, and you are therefore in real danger of forgetting it. This advice has the sound of a jest—until you meet someone who has in fact forgotten his or her name. People in this pitiable condition feel they have lost their identity, torment themselves with guilt, and have no occupation save to find someone who can tell them who they are.

While you're at it, write down the names of all the family

members you can remember, including those you feel confident you could not possibly forget. Keep this list nearby and review it from time to time. Imagine the embarrassment you would feel on meeting (a century or two hence) a parent or spouse you could not address by name!

DON'T volunteer to tell people the story of your death or ask them to tell you theirs (unless they're newcomers as well). The death experience is a thrilling novelty to you. To the rest of us, frankly, it's a bore. Remember that, with the possible exception of the Adepts, every single person you meet in the Afterlife has gone through it.

DON'T be offended if strangers suddenly take an active interest in what you're doing. This takes some getting used to, but you *will* get used to it. The rules of privacy here are different from those you knew in life. Let's suppose, for example, that you've found a storefront that appeals to you as a living space; a passerby, seeing you at work putting up a blind, will come in and without a word of greeting or introduction give you a hand. When you're finished, he may depart, again without a word, or he may sit down and make himself at home for the next few days. To feel outraged by this is pointless, and treating the intruder with icy disdain will probably have no effect whatever. On the other hand, good manners do not require you to entertain him; indeed, if you like, go somewhere else until he leaves.

Or let's say that you have just for the first time encountered the shade of your spouse and the two of you are busy sorting out a number of vexatious issues that were unresolved by death; a passerby will not hesitate to pause to listen or indeed to join in with complete enthusiasm. This sort of behavior may initially strike you as insufferable, but before long, believe me, you'll be doing it yourself. The social inhibitions you learned in life will not survive for long here.

DO leave your skin alone. This is not pleasant to say, but skin *does* present problems in the Afterlife, though they are not the ones you formerly knew—acne, pimples, drying, flaking, chafing, and so on. Take a moment, if you haven't already, to pinch your epidermis. You see? Looseness. On all Regulars (though not on Adepts) the skin is loose, though *prana* (rosy light) circulates throughout the channels of the corporeal residue, or "body." Tight-fitting clothes don't help. Nor do clothespins, paper clips, or staples, should they be available. Nothing, in the end, helps. Your skin is loose, that's a fact of the Afterlife, and I'm afraid I must not conceal from you the additional fact it *can* simply slip off entirely. This is exceedingly rare,[1] and it does grow back eventually, in most cases. If

[1] Also, you will be relieved to know that your chances of becoming one of the skinless is infinitesimally small. Figures taken, respectively, from J. Fardoust, *Epidermal Fashions and Trends,* and from R. N. Dhareshwan, *Implications of Horizon Accumulations Including Epidermal Deposits and Bone Simulacra,* report a ratio of 1:1,000,031, from a sampling of 1,991 Regulars (3% statistical error possible).

you travel for long, you will inevitably encounter skinless ones on the road, heads down, often in bands of ten or twenty, moaning or chanting one of their traditional laments, attributed to various sufferers in ancient and modern times, such as Petrus Comestor, Paramo, Geoffrey Chaucer, Victor Hugo, and Sir Edward Burne-Jones.[2]

---

[2] The skinless are not by any means universally considered to be objects of pity. They enjoy a sense of deep community that is rarely found in other segments of the Afterlife, and, contrary to what you might expect, their condition is neither painful nor hideous (at least to them).

CHAPTER 3

NEIGHBORS
IN THE AFTERLIFE

EVEN THE MOST BEFUDDLED NEWCOMER WILL make two observations about the Afterlife almost at once. The first is that while most inhabitants look very ordinary, a large number resemble disintegrating mummies. These peculiar-looking individuals (one hesitates to call them "persons") are *Husks.* Be assured that what you perceive in the Husks is *not* your future. If you are not ALREADY a Husk (and you wouldn't be reading this if you were), you're NOT going to become one.

The second observation the newcomer makes is that even ordinary-looking inhabitants are "different" from people in life. A lot of them seem wild, manic, and almost terrifyingly exuberant. On the other hand, a lot of them seem subdued, self-absorbed, and more or less oblivious to their neighbors' actions or opinions[1]; newcomers often assume that this affective deadness is just the result of being *dead*; it's not.

Let's be clear about the situation here: It is simply a fact that in the Afterlife no one needs to impress anyone or make a living or get ahead or scurry to get as much out of life as possible. These are things that death has put behind us forever. People adjust to this reality in various ways, but most of them adjust to it in ways that make them subdued, self-absorbed, and more or less oblivious to their neighbors' actions or opinions.

Some people find this social environment bleak and depressing, some fit right into it, and some ignore it and carry on in their own individual styles.

REGULARS

You and I belong to the class called (for want of a better term) Regulars. Again, I know that you belong to this class for the simple reason that you're reading this book. It may be fairly said that Regulars are what most people "expect" to become after death (provided that they have any expectations at all in this regard). This is of course a matter of memory. What we Regulars remember is that, in life, everyone was more or less "like us."

---

[1] The contradiction between this observation and the warning in the preceding chapter is more apparent than real. You will find your neighbors to be *both* intrusive *and* oblivious—even, sometimes, simultaneously.

Everyone looked like us, moved like us, felt like us, thought like us, and so on. As far as we're concerned, Regulars look "ordinary" and even "lifelike." It has been pointed out[2] that this might well be an illusion or false memory. Perhaps when Husks compare themselves to the living (if they are capable of doing such a thing) they too seem "ordinary" and "lifelike." Perhaps the living are in fact more like Husks than we remember them.

You will quickly notice that persons of every age, sex, and race can be found among the Regulars—with the very notable exception of infants and very small children. A number of theories have been proposed to explain their absence. Rutger Stanley,[3] for example, points out that "In ages before the appearance of the concept of 'childhood,' it was generally supposed that small children were not truly or fully human at all. Some thinkers went so far as to suggest that they formed a kind of pupal species distinct from our own." By contrast, V. A. Broadhurst[4] feels that, "in consideration of their manifest innocence, the souls of small children must surely occupy some state nearer to the paradisaic than our own." Another theory is mentioned in the following section.

---

[2] For example, by A. H. Delver in *Demythologies* (1957).
[3] In *Forest of a Thousand Ghosts.*
[4] Quoted in S. B. Beckett's *The Life of Afterlife.*

HUSKS

Husks will be found stacked in disused areas everywhere—against a road sign, a cucumber cellar, a lean-to. Their condition—of emptiness, lightness, fragility—has been attributed to various causes. Ramagadri is confident that "in life they were aspirants to the highest (seventh) level." Claudel suggests that "those who die in infancy project into the Afterlife eidolons or weak images of what they would have become had they lived to adulthood; these eidolons are without doubt the Husks that we see everywhere; they are adult in size but necessarily empty." Claudel's conjecture seems to many to be confirmed by the fact that the faces of Husks are invariably expressionless and without character—devoid of any normal traces of habitual thought and emotion, such as frown- or laugh-lines.

Husks soon disintegrate—"like fallen leaves," as the poet Tennyson has put it. That one must move more or less perpetually through a litter of whole or dismembered Husks is a fact of Afterlife to which one must become inured if not altogether indifferent. Count yourself fortunate that it is left to the Adepts to dispose of the remains.

ADEPTS

The Adepts represent one of the true enigmas of the Afterlife. The received wisdom regarding them is that, unlike all other inhabitants, the Adepts have never enjoyed an earthly existence; in other words, they are not the *formerly alive* but rather the *never-*

born. I call this "received wisdom" but am unable to say from whom it is received; unless it was in some far ancient time, it did not come to us from the Adepts themselves, for they do not teach, write, or even speak to us (though it is evident that they understand our own speech).

The Adepts are embarrassingly superior to us in many ways: unflaggingly cheerful, gracious, helpful, simple, childlike. They cannot be provoked to anger or impatience by any known means. At the same time, their saintliness is utterly unflavored by character; they are individually indistinguishable one from another, like handsome, sexless dolls all cast from the same mold.

It is generally assumed that the Adepts are souls "waiting to be born" in human form. At conception (according to this theory), they naturally disappear from the Afterlife. If they are aborted, stillborn, or die in early childhood, they return to the Afterlife as Husks, which are, after all, very like Adepts in one respect: They are like *ruined,* sexless dolls all cast from the same mold. If in life they survive childhood, however, Adepts soon achieve "the true character of humanity" (as Rasmussen puts it), which means that they thereafter sooner or later arrive in the Afterlife as *us* (the Regulars). No practical way of testing the theory has ever been devised.

LUNATICS, ECCENTRICS, AMNESIACS, AND MEMORY-LOSS HYSTERICS

Many a newcomer's first impression of the Afterlife is that it's not much different from a madhouse. Be assured that—as you become accustomed to what you see (and as your own values and behavior change)—this impression soon fades.

Except for eliminating purely biochemical disorders like depression and schizophrenia, death does not automatically change anyone's personality. Neurotics remain neurotic, the small-minded remain small-minded, and the deranged remain deranged. Severe derangement is a crippling condition in life, where one must obtain food, shelter, and other necessities (usually in cooperation with others); in the Afterlife the severely deranged person is, quite frankly, no worse off than anyone else. In fact, there is no reason to suppose that persons who seem deranged by "normal" standards are less happy or less "well off" than anyone else. Indeed, the very notion of normalcy is virtually meaningless in the Afterlife.

Many of those who strike newcomers as lunatics are simply old hands who long ago gave up caring what anyone thinks of them. They may have been extremely conventional people in life, but here they caper and bray and declaim and cavort, as pleases them. Before long, as inhibitions wither, you may well find yourself doing the same.

People will often alarm newcomers by proclaiming that they've forgotten who they are. It was long assumed that this was a sort of "hazing" that people like to put newcomers through. In modern times, however, this has come to be viewed as a more complex activity. It's true that some people will tell you that they've forgotten who they are simply to tease and frighten, but it has been shown that others do this because they're *worried* about forgetting who they are—and only newcomers are willing to listen to their anxieties. Still others have let their worries on this score become confused with reality; they're genuinely doubtful of their own identity and often have no way of confirming it.

Be warned that (unless you're a very steadfast isolate) you will sooner or later find yourself in the vicinity of an outbreak of memory-loss hysteria. It happens this way: One individual in a crowd suddenly announces that he has "gone blank," alarming others around him and causing *them* to go blank. A widespread chain reaction occurs like lightning, creating the strong impression that everyone in the crowd has been simultaneously struck "memory-dead," by some hostile cosmic force. Instead of rapidly dispersing, as might happen in other stressful situations, the crowd "implodes," seeking reassuring contact; this naturally has the effect of intensifying and prolonging the effect, which can last for hours and even days. Eventually boredom overcomes terror, the crowd drifts apart, and people bit by bit begin to reassemble their identities.

Most people, on being surprised by an occurrence of memory-loss hysteria, will succumb the first time, no matter how often you warn them to be on their guard against it. It takes real presence of mind and strength of character to instantly begin to shout out, "I know who I am! I know who I am!" until you're free of the panic-stricken crowd, but nothing works better (and may inspire others around you to save themselves as well).

GREETERS AND OTHER DUBIOUS FRIENDS

In Afterlife as in life, newcomers are always apt to be taken advantage of by people who have been around for a while. These old hands are not necessarily vicious people; on the contrary, those whose motives are the most benevolent are often the most troublesome.

Greeters (or as some call them, *Mentors*) would like to "take you under their wing" or "show you the ropes." They may be sincere, well-meaning, and truly helpful people, or they may be desperately lonely and needy people who would like to make you dependant on them. Whatever the case, if they hint that they are in a position to "pull strings" on your behalf, be warned that they are either deceiving themselves or attempting to deceive you; billions have looked for those strings, and they're just not there to be pulled.

Money lenders will offer you cash at trifling interest rates or even at no interest, alleging that you will be helpless without it or that it will enable you to achieve a better start in the Afterlife. The money (always gorgeous to look at) is completely worthless and without use. Surprisingly enough, however, your easiest course is simply to accept it. Knowing the money is worthless, the lender has no desire to get it back or to collect the equally worthless interest. Why then does he offer it in the first place? Who knows? Perhaps to achieve a momentary feeling of importance, to win a smile of gratitude, or just to pass the time.

Finders will volunteer to track down your loved ones. These, for the most part, are harmless romantics who in life dreamed of being Sam Spade or Philip Marlowe. Having nothing better to do, they betake themselves here and there in the Afterlife, supposedly looking for your missing friends and relatives. Sometimes they find them; more often, alas, they just lose interest and disappear.

Mediums will tell you that they are able to put you in touch with the living. As in life, there are those who believe in these claims and those who don't. Wieland notes that "several (disputed) methods of how the dead communicate with earth have been 'documented,' but we must once again emphatically state that the message sent is never the message received, the code is always absent, the signified a travesty of the signifier. For example, a philosopher in our neighborhood claims when he tried to send Wittgenstein's elementary statement *Die Welt ist alles, was der Fall ist* (The world is everything, that is the case) to his troubled daughter, it appeared in her bathroom mirror as THROW AWAY THE LADDER AND THEN CLIMB UP IT. Granted, one may be amused by these 'communications,' but interest in this game soon wanes."[5]

Erotogogues will show you the way to astonishing sensual pleasures. They cannot fulfill their promises; no one and no thing can, here in the Afterlife. A desire lingers (why else would you still be interested in this subject?), but it's neither strong nor long-lasting. Should you be tempted by their talk, I suggest you ask for specifics and then watch them blush, fidget, stick their hands in their pockets, begin to whistle, look about as if they had

[5] Naturally, the philosopher had to wait until his daughter arrived in the Afterlife to learn what message she had actually received.

40

suddenly forgotten something that demands their immediate attention, then see how they gradually walk backward until they disappear, humming and whistling all the while, into the nearest wall.

Hired Guns will locate your enemy and turn him into a husk. Ah, if only it were so. The pleasure of belated revenge! All the abuses you suffered at his or her hands. The time he held your face in the dirt and made you eat it. The physical education teacher who, while you were running track, told you to wipe that smile off your face. The one who made you tremble in front of your girl. The one who lied. The doctor who told you to keep smoking, that a cure for cancer would be found before you died. The one who wrote "due to exigencies beyond our control." The one who said, "I don't like the way you breathe." Ah, these and others, so many others. What a treasure! What an orchard of enemies to choose from!—But wait. What is the fate you wished on them? That they were dead? Well, they are, or will be soon enough. And of course they can no more be turned into Husks than you or I.

TAKE IT TO HEART: DON'T WORRY, BE HAPPY

When newcomers realize that the Afterlife is not a community of saints, they often become anxious for their personal safety, privacy, and general well-being. They wonder how they can protect themselves from their neighbors without the support of laws, courts, and police. Once again, it is the universal experience that the habitat accommodates itself to local needs. To take a

41

very mundane example, let's suppose that someone in your immediate vicinity is bothering you with noise. Even if no one else is bothered by the noise, the habitat will react locally to relieve your distress. This might occur in a variety of ways. Perhaps some sound-blocking barrier will be interposed between you and the noisemaker. Perhaps you will come across more attractive quarters elsewhere. Perhaps the noisemaker will find more attractive quarters elsewhere. Perhaps whatever mechanism is actually producing the noise will fail and be replaced by one that is silent.

"But what," you may wonder, "has become of the psychos, the lunatics, the mad slashers, the serial killers who have been sent to us in such large numbers in recent decades? Aren't they here somewhere, lurking in alleys, skulking in doorways, hiding in attics?" It takes some time, but you will eventually realize once and for all that you *cannot come to physical harm* here in the Afterlife. People can irritate you with their presence (or with their noise, as in the previous example), but they cannot restrain you or injure you. (This is not because *they* are ghosts but because *you* are a ghost; Jack the Ripper would get no more satisfaction from taking a knife to you than he would from taking a knife to a swarm of mosquitos—and he's well aware of it, wherever and whoever he may be.)

ALL THE SAME, THERE ARE NUISANCES

This is undeniable and unfortunate, but what is one to say about it? Some people feel that "Rest in Peace" should constitute an Afterlifetime guarantee, but to whom can one complain or demand a refund? Facts are facts, or have been from the earliest times—literally millions of years ago—to the present.

Stalkers, crazed worshipers, and unwanted lodgers operate in the Afterlife in exactly the way they did (and presumably still do) in life. They hang around their victims, trail them wherever they go, invade their privacy and peace of mind, and burden them with menace, with unwanted adoration, or simply with their presence. Although those who were celebrities in life are more attractive to these pests than others, anyone can end up with one, and the question then becomes, what to do? Since there is no court to enjoin them from troubling you, you must find and implement your own solutions. Most often, victims simply leave, go on an indefinitely extended walkabout, and hope to wear out or leave behind their tormentors. Sometimes it works, sometimes it doesn't.

In fact, if a really persistent nuisance of this sort attaches himself or herself to you, only an Adept can offer any genuine hope of effective assistance. Approach any one of them and explain your situation fully and frankly. The Adept will nod reassuringly, depart, and soon return with a band of four or five of his/her fellows, who will thereafter simply *surround* the person who is bothering you. From this point on, your tormentor will have to struggle to maintain a glimpse of you; he will spend every moment virtually smothered in the delicate, sticky sweetness that the Adepts exude. If six Adepts are insufficient to screen him from you and you from him, dozens will be found—hundreds. The Adepts will not tire of this task or become discouraged, even if it takes decades or centuries to persuade your persecutor that life might be more rewarding somewhere else than in your

43

shadow. When he departs at last, so will the Adepts, glazed smiles in place, without pausing to accept your thanks.

Some inhabitants of the Afterlife believe that this extraordinary ability and willingness of the Adepts to restrain, subdue, and reform malefactors is their entire reason for being. Some suggest that this activity is precisely what the Adepts are named for—this is what they are adept *at.* All this may be so. Should you ever (God forbid!) have need of their services in such a case, however, you must be prepared for the fact that, for as long as it takes, the cure is nearly as excruciating as the disease!

GUILDS AND CLUBS

Much of the energy that in life went into building families, businesses, and careers now goes into guilds and clubs. Guilds tend to be intense, all-absorbing activities, often of a religious character, while clubs lend themselves to the exercise of hobbies. Guilds are stable, monolithic, and ubiquitous; if you join the Diggers here, you are automatically a member of this selfsame guild everywhere and everywhen in the Afterlife. Clubs, by contrast, are ephemeral, individual, and local (though they are of course free to form associations with other clubs); in other words, joining a chess club here (wherever "here" happens to be for you) doesn't enroll you in every chess club in the Afterlife. Individuals often belong to many different clubs but seldom to more than one guild.

One hundred thirty-seven guilds are active in the Afterlife at this time. All are described in detail in Akito's *Cyclopedia of Guilds*. A few of the most famous are:

- The Karroum (the skinless), very charismatic and very secretive, counting among its ranks such notables as Hatshepsut, Pythagoras, Æthelred I, Martin Schongauer, Anne of Austria, Marcello Malpighi, Claudio Monteverdi, Herman Melville, and Sarah Bernhardt.
- The Guild of the Dark Brother (see Chapter One), one of the oldest and most powerful (in the sense of being attractive to the dead of every age) in the Afterlife. Guild members are engaged in "the search for the Dark Brother," a highly evolved mystical pilgrimage, physical and spiritual, that will end when the Afterlife itself ends.
- The Society of Fools, which describes itself as "The Biggest Traveling Show in the Universe." Its members are not only entertainers of every type (clowns, comics, jugglers, magicians, dancers, acrobats, singers, and so on) but musicians, librettists, dramatists, acting troupe, poets, painters, storytellers, novelists—indeed practitioners of every art known. It is a heartfelt byword of the Afterlife: "Where would we be without the Fools?"

"The Acropolis" becomes a staging area for players of the Society of Fools as they ready themselves for a traditional January performance of Aristophanes' *The Frogs*, this time in modern dress. The Parthenon seen in the background was reconstructed (as a ruin—rather absurdly, in the view of many), at the instigation and under the supervision of Thomas Bruce, 7th Earl of Elgin (1766–1841), the very man who in life despoiled the original of its most magnificent sculptural decorations (the so-called Elgin Marbles).

CHAPTER 4

THE AFTERLIFE
AS A HABITAT

THE ROAD

The Road, with its various branchings, dominates the geography of the Afterlife, if only because it seems central to all our goings-on. How do I find the Central Registry? you might ask a passerby, and she will inevitably respond, Follow the road and take the third (or fourth or fifth) branching.

When you awake (assuming you are one of those who sometimes sleep, as opposed to the sleepers who sometimes, though not always, wake), you will step out of the alley, bedroom, lean-to, wherever you were reposing, and find yourself, no matter how evocative your dreams were, back on the road.

Think of it how you will—as the route that will take you from place to place in the Afterlife, as the way (i.e., The Way into the next realm, if you believe in such), or as a path through infinity or the road to nowhere—regardless, it is there, this ash-colored line that divides the hamlets, the towns, the cities, the vacant fields where it is edged with shallow ditches. It's there, so why not use it? You'll find you have, after all, little choice in the matter.

It is possible to become obsessed with the road. Shades are often seen staring at it from a distance or cursing it or even on their knees praying that it lead them where they wish to go, most often to the end.[1] But the road is not a conscious entity, it is a road, nothing more, and will not answer prayers.

In the galleries you may be surprised by the number of paintings that depict the road; it's not (I think) a disproportionate number when you consider that we see it almost everywhere we

---

[1] See De Selby O'Brien, *The Life and Afterlife of De Selby O'Brien.* De Selby's analysis of the road in his chapter, "The Road and How I Rode My Bicycle Up and Down It to Eternity and Returned to Tell the Tale But Forgot It Before I Could Write It Down," is by far the most detailed of the various accounts of how one can spend one's afterlife on the road. Written as an old-fashioned picaresque, De Selby recounts his encounters with the Singing Ray, the Wings of Fiery Desires, the Astral Light and Its Minions, the Hole in the Road that Leads to the Other Side of the Other Side, and so on, all adventures that no one, of course, has verified. Of the many source books he cites, none of them will be found in our bibliography, because they simply do not exist. However, before one entirely discredits De Selby, one should remember that his book is far more richly and realistically documented, than, say, Hatchjaw's *The Road's Wrinkles.* Alas, we cannot question De Selby about his adventures because shortly after completing his book, a wind storm left his brain in a shambles and he now believes himself a bicycle.

turn our eyes. None of our artists, by the way, paint portraits. Abstract paintings, yes, landscapes and abstract landscapes, but no portraits; I'm told a relative newcomer by the name of Barthes has produced a brilliant (though largely unintelligible) study of this curious phenomenon.

Although perhaps not a very graceful metaphor, it can truly be said that the road serves as an anchor in the After-life. There are times when our (presumably psycho-reactive) environment flutters and breaks down, our perceptual reality evaporates, as if, to quote Dr. Fat in his *Cantata 140,* "the mechanism by which the habitat is maintained has clicked to the off position." The buildings tremble, the "air" shimmers, and everything dissolves to an unfocused pall, leaving nothing of the habitat as we know it except the color of the air and, yes, *the road.*

The ancients are fond of telling the tale of the road's ori-gins—how once Nirmanakaya espied a snake and chased it down a road but when he caught up with it, it wasn't a snake but his mother's hair, so he bent down to pick up his mother's beautiful black hair and return it to her, but when he picked it up, it was a crack running across the earth and this crack was the road he was standing on, and before it could swallow him up he tossed it high into the air, so high it went past the moon, so high it went past the stars, so high it left the universe altogether and landed in the Afterlife where ever since it has led pilgrims to its end.

Of course there is no end to the road, or at least no one has given a believable account of it (see footnote 1 in this chapter). Still, many like to believe in an end, and you will see them walking down it in droves. Juanita Zend[2] in her only postmortem work to date posits a circular road so vast in length that to the eye it appears to be straight. In her study she cites the testimony of one hundred road watchers who claim to have seen travelers set off in one direction in search of the road's end and then *reappear* centuries later, coming from the opposite direction. As is to be expected, when informed that they were passing the precise spot where their journey had begun so long ago, these travelers universally denied it and continued on their way.

What else can we tell you about the road? Let us simply reiterate that it is there, is hard on the feet and ankles as one walks down it, seems to fade away well before the horizon, and leaves layers of fluffy gray dust on our hands and clothes.

[2] Ms. Zend began her life as a child of parents unknown and later became Cincinnati's most respected chiropractor. After coming to the aid of a Colombian diplomat (she foiled a mugging outside a so-called convenience store), she married him and moved south where she wrote eighty-nine juvenile novels about a Colombian parrot called Parrot; the Parrot series was popular at the turn of the twentieth century, but (for reasons that can only be explained by the whimsicality of the gods of literature) was never translated from her native language, the Zend. After her husband's death before a firing squad, she returned to her native country where she gained some local fame with her "1001" series of paintings of one thousand and one spiral galaxies. She died in a Chicago tenement at the age of one hundred, a virtual recluse completely forgotten by her once-adoring public.

WHERE DOES ALL THIS *STUFF* COME FROM?

To ask where all this "stuff" comes from—clothing, buildings, streets, indeed even this book—is just like asking, "Where does the Afterlife come from?"

This stuff *is* the Afterlife.

HOW DOES IT GET PRODUCED?

Again, this is just like asking, "How does the Afterlife get produced?" This is not to imply that the question is a foolish one. Far from it. Thinkers of every kind have struggled for countless generations to account for what we all know occurs here: *Things get produced and they get produced in a way that to a greater or lesser degree suits the needs and desires of the deceased.*

The "ground" is firm under our feet. How? Why? In ages past, people liked to answer this question by saying that God makes it so. Nowadays the prevailing answer is that we inhabit a sort of shared hallucination; in this hallucination, we "agree" that having firm ground under our feet is desirable. Traveling elsewhere, we may encounter another sort of people who collectively prefer another sort of footing, and if so we shall have to accommodate ourselves to a spongy or marshy or perhaps even liquid surface.

Desert dwellers produce a desert habitat for themselves in the Afterlife—a sort of generalized desert habitat. The same can be said of every sort of distinct people. Country folk produce a country habitat. Urbanites produce an urban habitat.

Whatever the habitat, its most important feature (for us as individuals) is that it accommodates itself to individual needs *locally*. For example, think back to the way in which *The Little Book* came into your hands soon after your appearance in the Afterlife. It wasn't handed to you as you passed through some "pearly gate" of legend. You arrived; you looked around, puzzled, seeking guidance. Perhaps you soon found yourself passing a news kiosk or a bookstore, and there it was. Perhaps you sat down on a park bench, and there it was sitting on the bench beside you. Perhaps it fell out of the pocket of someone passing by. Or perhaps someone handed it to you and said, "Here, you dropped this." Whatever the case, there was a need in your locale, and this need was filled by the apparently "natural" appearance of a copy of *The Little Book*. (You probably thought it was a lucky event, but in fact this "luck" didn't happen just in your case; it happens in *everyone's* case.)

But, you may ask, how was this need met before *The Little Book* came into existence? The answer is simple: It was met in other ways, most often simply by the appearance of a helpful stranger. Once *The Little Book* became available, the "helpful stranger" was less often needed.

PRACTICALLY SPEAKING, HOW DO I GET THINGS I NEED OR WANT?

Let's say, for the sake of discussion, that you were a fine artist in life. If you decide to pursue this occupation in the Afterlife, you will naturally need certain supplies. There are no directories like the Yellow Pages that you can consult; where then are you to get the things you need? The problem is easily solved: Start looking for an art supply store, and *one will be found* somewhere nearby; this is an example of the habitat accommodating itself to a localized need.

Do I mean that the store appears in a place where there was no store before? Yes . . . possibly. Or possibly not. After all, there are many artists in the Afterlife, and it's not unthinkable that you have simply stumbled upon a store that has been there for decades or centuries. Practically speaking, of course, the question is moot.

The store will probably be unattended; most stores are. Simply go in and take what you want. How does it happen that the store is stocked with the things you need? Again, you may as well ask, "How does it happen that the Afterlife itself is stocked with the things we need?" The modern presumption is, as I say, that the habitat is responding locally to your needs. When you later return for more supplies, more will be there for the taking. Perhaps by that time someone will be "manning" the store, simply as a pastime. Perhaps by that time other artists will be patronizing the store. Perhaps you and your newfound friends will want to open a cooperative gallery. If so, you will doubtless require special lighting fixtures; if you look around, you will soon find a store in the neighborhood that handles the sort you need.

DOES THIS MEAN I CAN HAVE ANYTHING I WANT?

Unfortunately, no. There are principles involved that are only partly understood but that can be applied with fair reliability. For example (to continue our fine-art theme), let's say that you wanted a painting by Rembrandt to hang in your living room. You might well find an art gallery in your neighborhood, but it's very, very unlikely that you'll find a painting by Rembrandt in its stock; it's impossible to say with certainty why this is so. Is it because no one actually *needs* a Rembrandt to hang in the living room? Is it because a Rembrandt painting is too specific an object? Is it because such a work would be "beyond the powers" of the habitat to produce?

Note that I call finding a Rembrandt in your local gallery "very, very unlikely"—not "impossible." In death, as in life, anything can happen.

Some people believe the habitat acts in accordance with rules of its own. They would say, for example, that we are "not allowed" to have automobiles or guns. The more common (and perhaps more enlightened view) is that the habitat responds to the *ambient* needs of the community as well as to individual needs. People on the whole would react negatively to the appearance of cars or guns in their midst, and this theoretically "overrules" any individual's desire for these things.

It is the general experience that trivial, absurd, or fleeting whims are rarely fulfilled in the Afterlife. For example, to refer to a question in an earlier section, someone with a yen to produce a new version of *Ben-Hur* would probably not come across an entire film studio equipped to realize this extravagant goal. The habitat seems to be governed by a sense of proportion that probably corresponds to the sense of proportion of the general populace. If people had long yearned to see a new version of *Ben-Hur,* and a film director appeared in their midst with just such a project in mind, who knows?

On the other hand, if one were seized by a desire to take up filmmaking as a hobby in the Afterlife, this person's habitat would undoubtedly soon provide the means to do so.

With experience, people soon develop a sense of what they can and can't expect in the Afterlife. For example, anyone who knows the ropes will tell you that, if it is your consuming passion to while away eternity in an edifice like the Taj Mahal, don't expect the Afterlife to provide it ready-made. If you'd like to *build* such an edifice for yourself, however, the materials will certainly be provided.

YOU SAID NO ONE "OWNS" ANYTHING IN THE AFTERLIFE. IF I BUILD SOMETHING, DOESN'T IT BELONG TO ME?

In life (at least in modern times) you owned what you could defend, either with your own strength or with the force of law; if someone broke into a house that you "owned," you could point a gun at him, throw him out, or call the police. None of these options are available to you in the Afterlife, so the question of ownership is ultimately moot.

If you build a house for yourself and a passerby decides he wants to share it with you, there's not much you can do about this. No one will come and remove him at your command (but see the section "All the Same, There Are Nuisances" in the preceding chapter).

ARTS IN THE AFTERLIFE

Are there concert halls and theaters? Is Mozart still composing? Is Shakespeare still writing plays? Where can I find copies of my favorite books? These are a few of the many questions newcomers ask about the arts.

One of the universal oddities of the Afterlife is that those who were famous in the arts in life seldom pursue them here. Shakespeare has written no new plays (to the gratification of those who still charge that he never wrote any in the first place[3]). Mozart does not compose (though rumor has it that Salieri still does). Among fine artists, few have ever picked up a brush or chisel in the Afterlife.[4]

It appears that those who are most keen for the arts in the Afterlife are those whose artistic ambitions went unfulfilled in life. Since no one needs to "make a living," there is little sense of

[3] It should be noted, however, that Francis Bacon and all other candidates proposed as authors of the Shakespearean corpus are similarly playless.
[4] A notable exception was Vincent van Gogh, who carried his painting frenzy into the Afterlife with scarcely a pause to collect materials, and in the same isolation he practiced in life. One day in the early 1960s (it is said) a newcomer interrupted him at work to say that he, the newcomer, had recently acquired a van Gogh at auction for more than two million dollars. The artist (who sold only one painting in his entire lifetime) regarded the speaker with a piercing stare, laid down his tools, and walked away, never to return. It is a fact that the cache of van Goghs left behind amounted to more than seventeen thousand canvases.

Unlike the majority of artists, who abandon their career in the Afterlife, René Magritte (1898–1967) has continued to paint. Instead of searching for new subjects, however, he executes the same one in each successive work. Without significant variation, Magritte again and again paints a portrait of himself at work, painting—while glancing over his left shoulder, as if to catch himself at work. Asked to explain, the surrealist master replies simply: "I'm smoking."

"professionalism" in the arts here. Art shows, musical shows, and dramatic shows are put together on an impromptu basis; many are not "put together" in any sense but simply occur spontaneously.

Musical instruments are made by individuals to meet their own needs and are also available in stores, in the ordinary way. Instruments found in stores are invariably "new" and are often of no more than mediocre quality. Naturally, instruments of earlier times were available in the stores, and some of these evidenced a higher degree of quality than corresponding examples of today. For example, stringed instruments of the seventeenth and eighteenth centuries are sought as treasures, though none have ever been found to bear the name of Amati or Stradivari (or indeed any signature at all).

You will never (for some unguessable reason) find the texts of musical or literary works of the past "ready made" in the stores. Instead, you must look for them in a library.[5] The texts found in libraries are reconstructions, assembled by individual readers or committees of readers, from memory. All the sacred texts (the Bible, the Koran, and so on) exist in assuredly complete and accurate editions, and the same can be said of all the major world classics. Lesser works are usually found in fragmentary or conjectural forms, but it is estimated that fewer than one percent of all books published since the advent of movable type have ever been

---

[5] Not always an easy chore. A library (which is to say, a collection of books, musical scores, or manuscripts) may be found in the corner of a lean-to, in a building that looks like a warehouse, or in an abandoned "diner" parked at the side of the road. They are usually unmarked and unattended.

reconstructed in the Afterlife. (I have held in my hands a copy of Thomas Morley's *Plaine and Easie Introduction to Practicall Musicke, set downe in forme of a Dialogue* (1597) but have never been able to track down John Stuart Mill's *Principles of Political Economy* (1848) in order to discover why it was thought sufficiently dangerous by the Roman Catholic Church to warrant inclusion in the *Index Librorum Prohibitorum.*)

Specialized libraries, dedicated either to works of a single type or to works by a single artist, can be found in clubs devoted to the reconstruction of such works. These clubs are avid for new members, with fresh memories. Ask around.

This brings us to what has become the Afterlife's most popular artistic pastime, candid photography. Other arts—painting, sculpting, musical performance, and so on—change little between terrestrial life and the Afterlife, but this is not the case with photography. The means of Afterlife photography are discinctly "otherworldly," which is why it's considered a separate art form from sublunary photography—and the only art form truly native to the Afterlife. (Some have even gone so far as to give it a name of its own—thoughtography—but this graceless neologism has never caught on.)

Photography in the Afterlife doesn't require anything like "real" cameras or "real" film. Anything will do that is fundamentally articulated to simulate the camera/film relationship. An ordinary breakfast roll will serve as a camera if you *use* it as a camera. Shove in a stone (the "roll of film"), point it at your subject, go "click," and the work is done. Remove the stone, leave it somewhere to be "developed" (almost anywhere will do), then return in a day or two to pick up your "finished prints."

It works, but how well it works depends on the photographer. Two cameramen standing side by side and clicking at the same subject at the same moment will obtain widely different results. "Good" photographers are essentially "lucky" photographers; they are consistently so, and are lionized for their success (more so, indeed, than artists in any other field). The examples in this edition of *The Little Book* are drawn from the work of Robert ("Paco") Culhane.

Afterlife shutterbugs are a breed apart, and it is a byword that, when the excitement of the Afterlife becomes too overwhelming for you, an hour spent in their midst will return you to a state of utterly stultified boredom.

PHANTASMS

Phantasms come into this chapter in much the same way they come into the ontology of the Afterlife: awkwardly. I've been told that a book in recent circulation among the living contains these weighty words: "Nothing unreal exists." Phantasms would seem to contradict this eminently reasonable doctrine.

Phantasms can be almost anything nonordinary, and anything you see that is nonordinary is probably a phantasm. If, for example, you come across the body of a hippopotamus, dead and bristling with arrows, in the aisle of a hardware store, this is undoubtedly a phantasm. If you come across a galvanized steel bathtub at the side of the road or a boxful of broken *Super Chief* china outside your door, these are very probably phantasms. Phantasms are distinguished by being insubstantial (more insub-

Wooden dog phantasm at the Crystal Tongue Gate—a typical example of the phenomenon; note the telltale absence of shadow. Anomalous images like the face peering through the gate are welcome accidents that, to aficionados, mark the work of good or lucky photographers; they become manifest only in photographs and are never visible to the naked eye.

stantial than the rest of the Afterlife), boring, and inutile in the extreme. Where do they come from? Folk wisdom says as much about their origin as anyone cares to know: "The road comes from below, phantasms from above."[6]

They soon disappear.

---

[6] In other words, the road is "solid," while phantasms are as insubstantial as the air.

CHAPTER 5
RELIGIONS
OF THE AFTERLIFE

PEOPLE WHO IN LIFE TROUBLED THEMSELVES TO
lead upright and abstemious lives on account of their religious
beliefs often feel disgruntled when they cross over and discover
that the lot of the pious in the Afterlife differs not a whit from
that of the most debased sinner. They feel cheated and are likely
to renounce religion as a sham and a trick. Indeed, religions that
in life promised "pie in the sky when you die" find few adherents
in the Afterlife. Religions that were primarily racial or ethnic or
social in nature have likewise not fared well.[1]

---

[1] I speak here of contemporary conditions, of course. Different conditions prevail in earlier
times. Take a "deep dive" and you'll come up in the midst of people whose view of reality is
animistic; for them, the transition between life and the Afterlife was a slight and unimportant

Nonetheless, religion is a powerful and enduring force among the dead.[2] The concerns and focus of Afterlife religions are different, naturally, from those of their earthly counterparts; none are morally prescriptive; none claim to be based on divine revelation or to have been divinely founded; none go in for proselytizing in any systematic way. Here there is nothing comparable to, say, the five pillars of Islam, the five observances of Judaism, the four yogas of Hinduism, the three vows of Buddhism, or the faith of Christianity. No one banters on about Atman/Brahman, Yahweh, Buddha, Allah, the Holy Trinity.[3] Salvation from the consequences of sin, original or otherwise, is no longer an issue. Charity, purity, and correctness of ritual observance are seldom pursued as ends in themselves. The

---

one; they perceive no great difference between the two, and so their religious beliefs are much the same as they were in life.

[2] Which is to say among the Regulars. Though they presumably have some sort of interior life, Husks are manifestly incapable of any activity that could be termed religion. Adepts take no interest whatever in our religions; many people assume they have one of their own that has no outward display whatever.

[3] Newcomers (for some reason especially theosophists) sometimes try to maintain the tradition they followed in life. For example, you might see a new arrival staring intently at a rock and then saying (paraphrasing Leadbetter), "Firstly, the whole of the physical matter is seen instead of a minute part of it; secondly, the vibrations of its physical particles are perceptible; thirdly is seen its astral counterpart composed of various grades of astral stuff whose particles are in constant motion; fourthly, the Universal Divine Life must be here in this rock although fifthly [here our newcomer pauses and appears deeply troubled] the rock is descending into the earth and the earth is descending into itself and I no longer can see the rock or earth." Then he will stand up, look questioningly at his surrounds, and never again quote (or misquote) his spiritual leader. A recently arrived theologian might try to start up a discussion on the fine points of the various arguments for the existence of God, but as soon as he mentions Anselm and the ontological argument or the arguments from first cause (cosmological) or design (teleological) or contingency, his listeners will shake their heads as if to say, "This we know already and all the counterarguments for whatever argument you may propose" and simply drift away.

Golden Rule, which in life could be pointed to as an underlying principle that all religions could affirm, has little practical meaning in the Afterlife.

It has never been an objective of *The Little Book* to provide a catalog of Afterlife religions. Even a cursory survey of them would occupy hundreds of pages. In any case, most newcomers have only one immediate question to ask about the subject: "What is expected of me?" and this is easily answered: *Nothing whatever is expected of you.* Probably half the inhabitants of the Afterlife have no religious connection or belief whatever. Another large portion, perhaps half of the remainder, regard religious activity as a form of ready entertainment, to be sampled at will, as books, films, or television programs were in life. Only the remaining quarter of the populace (to continue to speak in very rough terms) throw themselves into their religions with genuine belief and fervor.

In general, three kinds of religions are to be found in the Afterlife (again, as contemporarily experienced): *Crossing religions,* which, being based on faith in a life to come, more nearly resemble earthly religions than the others; *guild religions,* which draw together shades with similar interests and pursuits; and *spontaneous religions,* which are ignited unpredictably, burn brightly for a time, then (usually) disappear without a trace. In the Afterlife, it is not considered *de rigueur* to "belong" to one religion and shun all others. Shades who are inclined to religion tend to belong to all and to fill up their days attending one event or service after another.

CROSSING RELIGIONS

Newcomers are often surprised to encounter in the Afterlife a widespread and thoroughly respectable belief that some form of "crossing over" to "another life" still awaits us. The belief (which is not considered an inherently religious one) is certainly ancient, and may well be as ancient as humankind itself; no period has ever been visited in which it is absent.

The belief has two solid foundations in fact:

1. Crossing over to a different state of being has already occurred *once,* so why not twice? In life, it was easy to doubt the possibility of such a crossing; in the Afterlife, it is impossible to doubt it, for it has already happened. Additionally, believers argue with credible logic that a second crossing is clearly needed to fulfill our most ancient expectations: in the Afterlife, we are exactly *halfway* between beast and angel, *halfway* between the matter-heavy beings of earth and the matter-free beings of the spirit world. One more crossing, they assert, will surely bring us to the end of our journey. Nonbelievers reply: "What angels? What spirit world?"

2. People in the Afterlife *disappear.* There's no doubt about the fact; what is in doubt is its meaning. Believers are convinced that people who disappear have crossed over to a higher state of being. Nonbelievers take Occam's razor to this conviction, pointing out, quite correctly, that one need not do anything very unusual in order to disappear from one's normal stamping grounds in the Afterlife. One may simply walk away and never return. There are no police here to trace one's movements; there are no voter-registration rolls, no licensing bureaus, no data-

tracking systems of any kind. And, they further point out, many persons long thought to have crossed over have *returned*, giving one or another perfectly ordinary explanation for their absence. Believers reply that *some* of the missing have *never* returned—which of course is equally true.

Ramagadri devotes a whole volume (XXXIII) to the subject and observes, "If in fact there is another land or phase of existence to which we are destined to cross over, chances are good that many residents of that land or phase of existence believe that there is *yet another* land or phase to which they are destined to cross over. Even in death, there is no surcease to yearning in the human heart."

In life, the occasion for crossing over was not in question; if it occurred at all, it would occur at death. In the Afterlife, with death behind us, nothing is more in question than this: No future event presents itself as the obvious occasion for an additional crossing over. It is by their several answers to this question that crossing religions chiefly distinguish themselves one from another. Their theories of how, when, and why we are to find release from this stage of being are propounded in pamphlets that are handed out in the street, stacked in doorways, and scattered to the wind. There are hundreds of them. By ancient usage, all bear names suggestive of effulgence; if someone presents himself as an inhabitant of the Luminous Tower, as an associate of the Gleaming Eye Badger, as a scintilla of the Sheer Wing Luster, or as a rod of the Evanescent Bundle, you can be reasonably sure that the reference is to a crossing religion.

For nearly half a century, a group known simply as the Radi-ant has dominated the field, largely owing to their fortunate acquisition of "the Bodhisattva in Khaki." Their principal tracts, "The Thirteen Stages of Crossing Over" and "The Chant of the Khaki Bodhisattva," appear in Appendix I.

GUILD RELIGIONS

As the name suggests, guild religions are the religions of groups held together by common interests, pursuits, or conditions.

Karroum. The oldest guild religion is that of the skinless, who call themselves "the Karroum" and who call their religion by the same name (also spelled *Karrym* or *Kharrm*); the meaning of the word is unknown, though it may be an ancestor of the Sanskrit *Karma*, fate. The beliefs and practices of the Karroum are not discussed outside their ranks and are held secret from the newly skinless for many years, until it's certain that "recovery" is be-yond hope for them. The Karroum exert a powerful fascination over many minds, and their followers are virtually permanent attachments, so much so that they constitute a guild of their own (and practice their own secret religion).[4] The literature devoted to the Karroum and their followers is enormous.

---

[4] To add a generous measure of confusion, these followers, who are in fact completely intact, call themselves "the Skinless." Most people refer to the *truly* skinless as the Karroum, and reserve the term *Skinless* for their followers. When someone is said to be "as sensitive as a Skinless," this is a reference not to the Karroum but to their followers, who are notably captious and, well, thin-skinned.

The Penitents. In the Christian era, many newcomers arrived in the Afterlife believing it to be Purgatory and therefore adopted a life of prayer and penance in hopes of hurrying release to Paradise. Since self-denial of the usual kind (fasting, for example) produces little or no discomfort among the dead, they took to inflicting chastisements on one another. When the desired release failed to occur, people tended to get bored with this after a period of time (varying from years to centuries), and many defected to the catacombs (see below). The Penitents have declined steadily since the Middle Ages, but pockets of them can still be found here and there.

Catacomb Dwellers seek a great many different things, among them the Final Sleep, the Dark Brother, and Walling-In (or Reunion). There are not many "musts" in the Afterlife, but a visit to the catacombs, which are accessible nearly everywhere, is surely one of them. For those who have a taste for the macabre and the romantic, the catacombs are practically an alternative to the Afterlife itself. *Harsheult's Guide to the Catacombs* is comprehensive and always reliably up-to-date.

The Letheans. For most in the Afterlife, total and permanent memory loss is the Great Terror. For a Lethean,[5] it is the desired objective. Their beliefs and rites are centered on The Six, who "many centuries ago" achieved a state of total nirvanic oblivion. Unfortunately The Six cannot (for obvious reasons) explain how or when they attained this state. A careful distinction is made by

[5] Lethe, in Greek mythology, was a river in Hades whose waters cause drinkers to forget their past.

Letheans between "nirvanic" oblivion and the ordinary "street-corner" sort that can be encountered anywhere in the Afterlife. "Street-corner oblivion is indistinguishable from mere confusion and is a painful and distressing condition, altogether unlike the nirvanic."[6] It is said that The Six can be visited, though Letheans disagree about the rewards to be expected from such a visit; some claim that The Six are capable of transcendently illuminating discourse, while others insist that their amnesia is so sublime that they exist altogether without language. Needless to say, the pilgrim's route is a closely guarded secret.

The Dark Brother (see Chapter Three). This comes closer to being a universal religion of the Afterlife than any other, appealing equally to common folk and to intelligentsia.

SPONTANEOUS RELIGIONS

"Street-corner religions in the Afterlife," H. L. Mencken has written, "fall somewhere between rioting and television—less overwhelming than the first but far more entertaining than the second." Not much more can or needs to be said about them. They pop up, spread like wildfire, burn fiercely for a few months or a few years, then vanish. No stigma is attached to participating in any of them, no matter how bizarre the rite or how absurd the premise. In fact, they clearly satisfy a deep-seated human need for

[6] Helen Hansen Gable, *In the Waters of Lethe.*

communion with the bizarre and absurd. A few examples will give you the flavor.

The Densely Packed of the Central Realm. Whenever you see a hundred or more individuals swaying and moaning "Our Mistress, Our Mistress" over and over and holding one another close together, you know you have encountered the believers of the Densely Packed of the Central Realm. Their beliefs are founded on the following brief account:

Once a mosquito stung Our Mistress on the forehead, and the next morning she was dead. A woman in a flowing white robe took her hand and led Our Mistress along a wooden catwalk, then under a huge archway and up a staircase whose stairs were worn and sunken in the middle. At the top of the stairs was a balustrade where groups of the newly dead, still in their old physical forms, stared down at the sight beneath them. Our Mistress looked over the rail and saw the earth's globe in all its astonishing panorama spread out below her. Between the earth and wherever it was she was, the disintegrating forms of animals and human beings floated about in space. When Our Mistress looked behind her, she saw only a gray plane where dazed, shadowy human figures bumped into one another. Farther away others rushed about, scattering far and wide into the desert or clouds. Forms without faces or arms swam dreamily above the scurrying swarms. Suddenly a strong wind swept everyone and thing into one densely packed area and Our Mistress

71

asked the ear nearest her mouth where was she? Such tempests are not rare, the ear replied. Our Mistress felt the need to scratch furiously at her forehead, but when she attempted this, her forehead wasn't there. Her shell had fallen completely away, and, with the legions of the dead, she was dragged by the wind's appendages deeper into the hinterlands.

The Church of the Tachyonists. Not a church in any ordinary sense, but you'll see them gathered in the fields, perhaps a dozen members (whatever the number, it must be even). First, they will discuss their basic tenets, or rather not discuss, but stand in pairs and, in litany fashion, state them to one another, nodding enthusiastically all the while.

"We move so fast we don't move."

"Yes, yes."

"We move so fast we are not here."

"Yes, yes."

"We move so fast the light cannot know us."

"Yes, yes."

"We move so fast no one can detect us."

"Yes, yes."

"Can you see my hands move?"

"No, no."

"Can you see my eyes?"

"No, no."

"Am I even here?"

"No, no, no."

Then they will pull from the pockets of their tattered coats sheets of paper, which they roll into tubes. Into each tube a bead is placed, or if beads aren't available, a pebble or a pea. Then, with a member at one end of the tube and a member at the other, they blow the bead (pebble, pea) back and forth for several minutes, from one Tachyonist's mouth to another, until they seem to tire of their ritual. They unscroll the tubes, return the paper to their pockets, and the last ones to have beads swallow them. Then, almost as if they were embarrassed, they nod to one another, and wander out of the field and back onto the road.

Curiously, no Tachyonist claims to have seen the phenomenon of the "whales" (discussed in Chapter One) from which the physicists first derived their theory of tachyons constituting the base medium of the Afterlife.

The Church of the Afterlife as Will and Idea is among the oldest and most respected of the spontaneous religions (insofar as any of them can be said to be respected). Some believe it will ultimately achieve the status of a guild religion (in five or ten centuries). It's found in two forms, the Psycho-reactive and the Schopenhauer-influenced.

Adherents of the psycho-reactive persuasion hold that the Afterlife and its constituent parts are formed by the willing of it, that it is an environment that comes into being by reacting to our conscious and subconscious desires (Quine, Walmsey, et al.). To begin a meeting, they will knock some benches together, sit down, and decide what it is they want the Afterlife to be for the duration of their assembly (an Alpine meadow, a wintry southeast Texas beach, leaf season along Lake Biwa in Shiga Province).

73

The founding meeting of the Church of the Afterlife as Will and Idea
(Schopenhauer-Influenced), which split from the Psycho-reactive in 1901.
Schopenhauer himself is easily recognizable as the second shade from the right. At
his left sits James Russell Lowell, the American poet; at his right are the British
radical reform politician John Bright, Frederick III of Germany, American
Abolitionist leader William Lloyd Garrison, and Italian patriot Giuseppe Garibaldi.

They then proceed to "will" this form into being. What outsiders see, of course, is only a handful of thinkers sitting on wooden benches and holding their foreheads in intense concentration.

The Schopenhauer-influenced hold that the Afterlife and its constituent parts are formed solely by the perception of the perceiver, that these constituents have no substance in themselves, are merely perceptions. Objects exist only in relation to subjects. The Afterlife, to paraphrase Schopenhauer, is idea. All that in any way belongs or can belong to the Afterlife is willy-nilly conditioned through the perceiver, exists only for the perceiver, is only the perception of the perceiver, is, then, entirely perceptual. To begin a meeting, the Schopenhauer-influenced will knock together some benches, sit down, and decide what it is they are perceiving for the duration of their assembly. This done, they reflect on the fact that it is only perceptual anyway, so what does it matter? What outsiders see, of course, is only a handful of thinkers sitting on wooden benches and holding their foreheads in intense indifference to everything.

Two other religions of the spontaneous sort can be sampled in Appendix II.

CHAPTER 6

IN WHICH
LIES ARE EXPOSED!

NEWCOMERS TO THE AFTERLIFE—WHO ARRIVE full of alarm, confusion, and apprehension—turn to *The Little Book* for gentle reassurance and cold facts, and these are the principal fare of the early chapters. I assume that, since you've reached this point in the text, your own alarm, confusion, and apprehension have abated to a point where you can with equanimity hear a truth that I have systematically suppressed in earlier pages:

The Afterlife is *Hell.*

In your heart-of-hearts you knew that, didn't you?

On the other hand, it is no less true to say that . . .

The Afterlife is *Heaven.*

•   •   •

The doctrine of the Roman Church[1] will assist me in solving this strange paradox. As the theologians of this sect have worked it all out, one's disposition in the Afterlife is determined absolutely and solely by the state of one's soul at the moment of death: Die in a state of grace—even after a whole lifetime of debauchery—and you are Heaven-bound (though a bit of purgatorial polishing may be needed before you actually get there); die in mortal sin—even after a whole lifetime of angelic piety—and it's hell for you, once and for all.

Obviously an element of something very like luck determines your fate under this system. Be struck by lightning as you step out of the confessional box, and bliss is yours, forever. Slip in the bathtub and crack your skull while dismembering your spouse, and it's excruciating torment for a period longer than any of us can imagine. To increase one's chances for eternal happiness, one is always well advised to lengthen the odds: Just as a matter of raw statistics, the habitual saint clearly has a better chance of dying in a state of grace than the habitual sinner.

Thinkers of the Reformation and of later times were not at ease with this rather arbitrary approach to human fate in the Afterlife. Character—the state of one's conscience—seemed more to the point than a state of grace that could be produced almost mechanically with the proper sacramental formulas.

[1] If in life you were in need of a razor (and only the finest would do), you visited Kindal on the *avenue de l'Opéra* in Paris; if you were in need of an umbrella of a similar quality, you visited James Smith & Sons on Oxford Street in London. In need of a doctrine, where else would one turn except to the Church of Rome?

Gradually an altogether new vision of Heaven and Hell began to emerge: Heaven and Hell were not places to which people were *sent* in death, Heaven and Hell were places people *chose*—in life.

And thus is the paradox solved.

The Afterlife is full of people who made their life on earth a Hell. Why should they not do the same here? For them, the Afterlife is Hell because they brought Hell with them, and *wherever they are is Hell.*

You can verify this for yourself very easily. Visit a human monster, a Joseph Stalin or an Adolf Hitler; for tens of kilometers around them, you will find utter silence and desolation. They sit enthroned in the center of their own Hells of misery, loneliness, and hatred . . . forever. Forever not because some God has condemned them to it, but because they have condemned *themselves* to it. Hell is all that they know—all that they ever knew. If they wanted to, they could abandon Hell tomorrow—as they might have done in life . . . if they'd wanted to.

But the Afterlife is also full of people who made their life on earth a Heaven. They brought Heaven with them, and wherever they are is Heaven.

As in life, most of us live well within the polar extremes. Some of us were denied any real chance at making life on earth a Heaven for ourselves. A child who is sent to work in the mines at age five and dies before his tenth birthday has little chance to learn the language of bliss. The victims of war, slavery, and oppression come to us knowing little but Hell and have to develop an aptitude for its opposite. Wherever you go in the cities, across the deserts, in the catacombs, down the road that leads to forever, you'll see Heaven and Hell on every side . . . in *us*. Look for them and you'll soon know them. There on your left, Hell shuffles by, carrying a reluctant, gloomy chicken, his only comrade. There on your right, Heaven springs past, singing—a lunatic, a little too much for civilized contact.

Just the way it always was.

APPENDIXES

I'VE ALWAYS FELT I WOULD BE DOING LESS THAN my best for newcomers to the Afterlife if I were to include in *The Little Book* nothing but answers to their most obvious and urgent questions. A staggeringly enormous treasury of writings about the Afterlife—of every kind, including (but not limited to) the literary, the scholarly, the scientific, and the speculative—has accumulated over the millennia, and I like to conclude each new edition of *The Little Book* with a minute sample drawn from it.

In past editions, I have included:

- an account that comes to us from an African people (presumably of *Homo habilis*) so ancient that the Afterlife was, they claim, uninhabited by the human kind until they arrived

- Benjamin Franklin's "Six Improvements of the Afterlife Which Could Be Easily Effected by Its Inhabitants"
- an excerpt from Sigmund Freud's *The Psycho-Analysis of Joan of Arc*
- "An Admission of Error," written specifically for *The Little Book* by an unfortunately still crazed and unrepentant Adolf Hitler (seventeen words in German, twenty-one in the English translation)

The selections I've made for this edition come more nearly under the heading "Literary Curiosities and Popular Philosophical and Scientific Delusions."

TWO CROSSING-OVER TRACTS

WHEN A CROSSING-OVER PAMPHLET IS THRUST into your hand on a street corner or blown into your face as you trudge down the road, you will be forgiven for thinking of it as a piece of litter. Crudely printed, on the flimsiest available material, these dismal screeds seem designed to make a poor first impression. Nonetheless, some are very ancient texts that scholars would not hesitate to shelve alongside the Rig-Veda, the Three Pitakas, or the *Kojiki* and *Nihongi* of Japan.

The following description of the stages of crossing over is embraced by the Radiant, who meet in covens of thirteen on the thirteenth day of the first month of every thirteenth year[1] and chant their doctrine for thirteen hours. You may already have heard fragments of their "song" floating on the etheric currents.

THE THIRTEEN STAGES OF CROSSING OVER[2]

I.   You who know nothing of crossing over, listen carefully. This is the Stage of Symptoms, the bleeding through the nose, the sores, the illuminated head—when the spirit becomes enkindled and you cannot resist your quitting the body.

2.   In this mansion everything is different, everything causes afflictions. The light will not come back, though you shudder and complain. The knowledge-holders wait with their *lokas* of fatigue, wait and ripen with the dawn.

3.   Too long standing in one place brings the Flame-enhaloed Deities. Do not wince within their illusion, even though they are frightening. Keep alert. Those are fisheyes staring down upon you.

4.   The Dweller on the Threshold cannot help you. He is

---

[1] I should not have to remind the reader that the reckoning of time in the Afterlife is highly subjective. What is noteworthy in this connection is that the Radiant claim that their coven meetings occur like clockwork, without members being prepared or notified in advance. On the thirteenth hour of the thirteenth day of the first month of the thirteenth year, all spontaneously and simultaneously come together (they say).

[2] The first English translation of the Thirteen Stages was made by John Colet (1466–1519), a friend of Erasmus and of Thomas More. The author of this recent translation is unknown.

blind. Only the soul is aware that what it is experiencing is no hallucination. Pick up a bone relic and cross over.

5. Listen well to the Blood-draining deities' questions. Say: *I will give you an account of the state of heavenly water flowing through the thirteen mansions of the moon and how on a certain road I saw the sun set in a pool of black mud.* They will then be occupied forever with understanding.

6. Do not think this stage has to do with dreaming, that the soul is here made drowsy, neither asleep nor awake. You must bathe in the fire of the newly born if you are to escape this most miserable of stages.

7. In the dark substance the scintillae appear. Do not follow them. Follow instead the seven planets and their stars, though they too will lead you downward. Everything does, here in the holiest of paradises.

8. Learn to listen without distraction. There is continuity of sorts in even the darkest doctrine. Follow the path that's already established. The earth will offer no resistance. It will lead you to a pond where you pick Sentients like lice from your pores.

9. If you try to flee without thinking, the Blood-draining deities will sing you into their skull-bowls. Pain pervades you wholly. Axes whistle through first the right wrist then the left. A polished bell is placed in the eastern hemisphere of your brain and will ring and ring—if you try to flee from this stage without thinking.

10.   If you no longer recognize yourself in the maelstrom, head for the Cave. Enter with no expectation, muttering *thunderfist* over and over. Here the great treasure lies hidden. Here Hiranya-gabha awaits you with its six eyes and its yellow incubator where the jewel reposes, and its pestle to mortar your skull.

11.   Yes, each stage will deceive you, if you do not attend carefully. This is not an imaginary journey. He Who Is Truly Small will take you down to his own littleness. The larger shadows are not to be trusted.

12.   From horizon to horizon the sky trembles. The clouds disperse. Thought-forms float by as thick as trunks. The word *incarnate* separates from the spirit. This is the Twelfth Stage. You must learn to enjoy it. It will last for twelve periods.[3]

13.   Lost one, this is the Dawning of Radiances. You're lucky you made it this far. The owl will take you to the Four Females Who Keep the Door, where an opulence awaits you, and elephant, ibex, wolf. The Doorkeepers bite their nether lips. Their eyes are glassy. The head they lay at your feet is yours.

The most famous coven meeting of the Radiant in modern times occurred in 1951 in a storefront in Three Ponies.[4] The members

---

[3] Periods . . . of indeterminate length, presumably the equivalent of centuries.

[4] Three Ponies is held among the Radiant to be a veridical town, city, or crossroads whose location is well known (but never to the particular member of the sect you happen to be talking to). "Others know where it is," you will be assured. The following is a typical tale of this legendary place.

A certain man was walking toward Three Ponies when he met another coming from the opposite direction.

The stranger nodded in a friendly way and asked where he was going.

"I'm going to Three Ponies," he replied.

The stranger blinked in surprise. "That's odd," he said, "for I too am going to Three Ponies."

"It looks to me as though you've just *come* from Three Ponies."

"It looks the same to me with respect to you."

The two men stood for a moment in perplexed silence, then the stranger said: "I'm perfectly satisfied that Three Ponies lies ahead of me."

"I'm no less well satisfied that it lies ahead of *me*."

Further discussion of the matter seemed pointless, so each wished the other luck in his quest and went on his way.

Soon the man came to a small, dusty town. He kept on walking till he found its one hotel, where an old man sat on the porch.

"What is this place?" the traveler asked him.

"This is Three Ponies," the old man replied.

"Ah! I thought it must be. Have you been sitting here long?"

"All morning," the old man said.

"Then you may have seen a friend of mine walk through town." And he described the stranger he'd met on the road.

"Oh yes, I saw him," the old man said. "In fact, he asked me to tell you that he's waiting for you inside."

Flabbergasted, the man entered the hotel and immediately saw that the stranger he'd met on the road was sitting in the lobby.

"But how on earth did you get here ahead of me?" he demanded to know.

"I walked more quickly, of course."

"But you didn't pass me—I would have seen you!"

"Why would I want to pass you? You were going the wrong way!"

The man shook his head in bewilderment. "But that doesn't make any sense. I'm here, as you see!"

The stranger laughed. "Clearly you don't understand."

"You're quite right."

"Sit down and we'll discuss it."

The man did so.

"It's really very simple," the stranger said. "You can probably work it out for yourself."

"I don't see how. Going the wrong direction—according to you!—I arrived in Three Ponies. You, going the opposite direction, arrived in the same place ahead of me. I find it totally inexplicable!"

Smiling, the stranger shook his head. "You've missed the obvious."

"Please tell me what it is."

"But I've already told you—twice, in fact."

"What do you mean?"

"Didn't I tell you that you were going in the wrong direction to find Three Ponies?"

"Well, yes. Of course you did."

were nearing the end of their chant when the khaki-clad body of a young man crashed down into the midst of them from no-where—in the middle of one of his own sentences. Lying on his back in the dust, staring up sightlessly into the eyes of the shades around him, he continued to rave for about half an hour in a state of trance. At last he concluded with these words, "Did you make it? Is it over? Are you there?"—and vanished, never to be seen again in the Afterlife.

The astonished witnesses quickly reached the conclusion that this young man ("the Bodhisattva in Khaki") had in that very hour died, arriving in the Afterlife in a state of such advanced enlightenment that he was *already* uttering the directions he would need to follow in order to cross over to the next state of being beyond the Afterlife. In a panic-stricken frenzy, they began im-mediately to reconstruct the ranting words that had cascaded from his mouth.

To say that they were in a frenzy hardly covers the matter. They drove themselves into paroxysms of lunacy over the next two days, battling over what they'd heard in fact and in imagina-tion, interpreting sounds (did he say *lokas* or *logos* or perhaps *locusts*?), interpolating at whim and at need. They had been given (they felt sure) the most important revelation in human history, but how much of it did they have right? Not enough, evidently,

---

"And what do you conclude from this?"

The man stared at him in stupefaction.

"You went in the wrong direction," the stranger said, "and so you arrived in the wrong place."

"But this *is* Three Ponies!"

"Indeed it is," the stranger replied. "But *this* Three Ponies is not the *real* Three Ponies. You've made your journey for nothing."

for them to repeat the Bodhisattva's feat. Every year brings forth dozens of new attempts to "get it right." The version that follows makes as much (and as little) sense as any of them.

THE CHANT OF THE KHAKI BODHISATTVA[5]

First, your whereabouts.

Ask the old man on your left, the one supine in the gutter. He will tap-dance for fifteen minutes on a blue handkerchief then begin to bleed from the gums. Pick up the handkerchief and read it as if it were the last novel of a lost race known as man and if it says, "Through dominant freighters of imperial wardrobes," you know you're on the right track. Follow it.

Keep following it.

Those people, the ones whose faces are all alike, cluster with them in the corner for the dictation of simple transliterations, extraneous treatises fading in hands piping the sacred texts. Pay attention!

"The University."

"The Mortuary."

"The stiffening fingers."

Visit the Den of Winds.

How was it? Do you think you will ever come back again? Did

---

[5] The number given to this particular version is 403M. All versions numbered 403 are basically the same. The letter designation indicates that it was assembled after variant L and before variant N. The difference between lettered variants may be no more than a word or two.

the woman in the red swirl explain your shivers? Your sins? How much of life did you take in? 10%? 40%? 3%?

If you err at this stage, you will wander forever in "sangsara," so do not err, though your nerve endings are popping like balloons, like stars.

Take the bone-relics off the pyre and plant them. Soon tiny pigs will squeal forth from the ground. Kill them all and try to merge with their rainbow-hued blood. It is impossible, but you must try if you are to experience utter loneliness. The Purified Ones are calling.

Don't answer. Start jogging. This will keep you in shape for the later, more treacherous parts of the journey, like the mating with the scorpion or the swim through the mirror's smile.

Hitch up your dress or pants and start walking, it's not over yet. There are pits to be crossed and whole areas of "dilapidated air."

Are your fingers a dark yellow yet? Good. You are getting closer.

Mud raining from the skies, trees slipping from the bank, the days going backward and forward making whirlpools of the weeks. You are in another region, so wipe the smile off your mouth, here comes the blizzard of glass.

Follow the blind baby, your natural inclinations are useless now, and it will lead you into the desert where cars drift like lizards, their gaze filling you with dread—

—Palpable dread, plants, animals, motor brains.

"Sudden acts of physics seen intoxicated to immutable inceptions form continuity on radiated nails present set machine undoubtedly to the absorbent sky."

Bring this message to the technicians. They won't fix it, but will offer you a place to stay overnight and fortify you with tea. Thank them and move on.

The world is an invention, you think (how else could you have gotten out of the blizzard of glass?), but you are wrong. It is what it is.

Find out what day it is. The ninth? The tenth? The eleventh? If it's the eleventh you're in trouble so get out. Quick. Scram. Hurry. Make yourself scarce. Behind that rock, where the empty sacks sit waiting to be filled up.

Leave them alone. They're not really empty, but filled with poisonous dust. Can't you read? Head for the halo of flames.

"Ouch!"

Yes, it is difficult to put it out with your hands, but did you think your liberation would be easy?

Rock for an hour on the balls of your feet and Mother Ratna will speak to you in a vision.

"Here there everywhere blown around the middle."

Then she will point to the bean vine trailing away into the landscape and tell you to follow it. Don't. Go to a movie instead.

Go see *I Was a Deadman Adrift in a Cosmic Passage* playing at the Cameo in Magnolia, Arkansas. It's a bad film but you can obtain some much-needed sleep there.

Draw a deep breath, it will be your last, here is the coach that will take you to Tibet.

Thunder thunder thunder. It is winter. Girls in veils float through the streets. Don't worry if your clothes are impractical, if the wind whistles with ease through your ribs. Notice the man in the top hat with a boutonniere. What is he doing here? Probably the same as you; his fingers are swollen, too.

THE LAST BOAT IS NOW DEPARTING

Take it. No telling what would have happened back there.

In the Sacred Grove the nobly born are frying the tongues of busybodies and sucking clean their bones. Do not talk with them, these apostles of indolence. They don't know the way.

Can you feel your elbow smiling now? Your lungs rubbing against the clammy wall?

"The Doubtful."

"The Suggestive."

"The Double-layered."

Did you find out what day it is? The thirteenth? Then enter now the setting face-to-face.

Drink lustily from the skull-bowl; happiness is closer.

From the ceiling descend hundreds of miniature parachutists with their purple tumescent faces and their little knives. They scamper through your hair, your eyes. Lie quietly. You are in the condition of nothing-to-do, but it will pass. Here come the Buzzing Helicopters.

Here come the Buzzing Helicopters, don't just lie there, take off; they carry "lokas" with them that will cause you great pain.

You may suspend yourself in the silence, if you like, of the air-so-thick-you-can-cut-it.

Bridgeheads, temples, dotings, and hankerings.

"Rage."

"Despair."

"Stupidity."

THE DANGEROUS NARROW PASSAGEWAY

You are in it, the warm black ooze lifting you up under the arms. Tuck up your head and your knees, this isn't the path of good wishes any longer. And pay attention, damn it! Do you think this is a game? I could as easily lead you through the lobster priests, you know. Or put you through the glazing ceremony or the river of twitching.

Facts and rumors, who cares which at this point with the dancers vaporizing all around and ancestors feeding like fetuses on your flesh. Would you let them dehydrate?

"We're not talking tonight."

"Are we singing?"

Smells drift in the dark. At the borders red eyes reappear.

YOU ARE NEARING THE GREAT SYMBOL

That's right, the signs don't lie. You are nearing the great symbol. Close your eyes and hang onto the body-aggregate. Whoever is to be freed from the ambuscades must offend the madmen with a like madness.

Watch out for the wall of green jelly! Can't you see? Then open your eyes. And pay attention! This is it. Here we go.

Past slate houses stacked on hills, ladders angling out the windows, pervaders and knowers waggling wombs at the door. Ignore the interrupters. Concentrate on the red light ahead. The conditions are collapsing. Gestures, bridles, homunculi afloat in the black water.

"The heart drops."

"The three times."

"The secret doctrines."

Hazard no thoughts; begin the process of untalking.

In the invocation to the seven sattvas the body crumbles, the mind slips into its nest, the eyes into their cages.

The fingers fall; the feet dissolve.

Now through the mirror, now through the smile.

Wave after wave after wave . . .

Well?

Did you make it? Is it over? Are you there?

APPENDIX II

Two Spontaneous Religions

THE NAY-SAYERS

Led by Rev. Leo Bernhard, formerly a wine presser from the Neckar Valley, the Nay-Sayers meet in a "public" building (all buildings are public, of course, but they don't all *look* public). After a few preliminary remarks by the Reverend pertaining to the issues of negation, a member of the congregation will rise and come forth to state his or her piece, not unlike, say, what one used to find at meetings for the alcohol addicted in the previous realm. Also in the manner of an AA meeting, only the "elect" are allowed to be present, and these, as their "brother" or "sister" speaks, shake their heads rapidly back and forth, apparently in joyous negation of what they are hearing.

The following transcript of a young female Nay-Sayer was recorded clandestinely by Braz Cubas, formerly a gaffer for an independent film company based in Tampa, Florida:

I'd rather not, thank you. No. No, I am not ready. Don't ask me again, please. No, the trip does not seem worth it despite the shuffleboard tournament. The bullet can stay right where it is, thank you. You do not want me, I assure you. I am too young for your army. I will not sign. That simple? Of course it's not that simple. Your first concern is not my first concern. No, I won't tell you. I can't help it. I will not drink that water. Do you think I'm an idiot? I will not visit you, marry you, take you to Costa Rica. Your cuspids do not interest me. I do not practice zik-e-ruhe, tai chi, or rastafari. No. Thank you, no. I do not want to eat dinner. I don't care about lentil pâté. No, I don't want to see that movie. I did not get off at Alameda. The truck did not continue north on I-25. I did not pull the trigger. The bullet did not lodge in my skull. I will not cite studies of Indian tribes in Mexico or the rural inhabitants of Appalachia or certain groups in the Andes Mountains in Ecuador or the Hunzas in the Himalayas who live unusually long, healthful lives. I do not want a Naples biscuit, thank you. The staghound did not slobber on the rug at my feet. I did not turn away when, with a trembling voice, the boy whispered, "Cockles." Now was not the time for the arrival of Don

95

Bedaya dressed in his velour robes. Never have you heard
me say, "What sagacity!" I am not happy you have come.
I did not know Roland was also here. I do not give a fig
for Roland. I did not take this long without good reason.
I did not need to purchase books to pursue the subject.
My heart is not filled with joy. The dwarf did not turn,
stagger, collapse to his knees. Autumn was not rather
advanced. No, I do not find this particularly funny. That's
not the point. On those trips she did not seek or find
lasting serenity. I am not, sorry, an apostle of Hebbel.
The young serving girl did not begin to fill each bowl
with soup. Her dreams were not chaste. No, I do not
wish to attend your free intensive workshop wherein I
might discover my hidden potential, improve my self-
confidence and self-discipline, attain inner peace, achieve
personal goals, learn to relax and be happy. Thank you,
no. I will not go to the gardener's house where the ladies
are chatting. I will not pray. I will not join you in silent
prayer. I am not in a fool's paradise. I cannot tell you.
No one would relish a joke like that if he were the butt
of it. The poet did not pause for a moment to reflect on
the wisdom of his words. This is not Florence water. I am
not repeating myself; it is not necessary. These fresh
beginnings did not lead me into a new intellectual world.
When I entered, I did not see distress in her eyes. I am
not distressed by dullness or the lack of it. These are not
strange songs. I am not untroubled. It does not please me
to say this. I did not see that the child's parted lips were
tremulous. "Well, well," the Duke did not cry petulantly.
You are not invited. My time is not come. I did not
interrupt him with an ironic tone. The President is not

asleep. No. Absolutely not. You certainly may not. Nor
may I. You shouldn't think so. You shouldn't be seen
around here for the next one hundred years. Take it
elsewhere. You may not say I said that. The incident with
the cow is not an isolated one. The President is not at
home. No, I don't know where he is. No, Eglamore did
not run him through and give vent to a strangled,
growling cry. No, I am not done with this. The car did
not start up. I am not waiting for you. My eyes do not
follow you as you walk away. I am not feverish. No, thank
you. Thank you, no. I said No. You are not right. I am
not going away anytime soon. You can forget it. It's not
my problem, thank you.

THE CHURCH OF CONSTANT CRISIS

The popularity of this particular street-corner religion is inexplicable, but followers in abundance it has. They fill the auditorium,
they hang from the balcony, they cram the aisles. But to do what?
Well, to participate in a bipartite service that begins with a
Sermon of Interrogatives:

What are the issues? Are they clear? Are there parameters?
What do they look like? Mountains in the distance? An
island surrounded by an ocean? Whales? Does the
possibility there are no parameters help establish
parameters (albeit illusory) we might work within to come
to terms with the crisis, if not solve it altogether? What

Members assemble in the Liverpool Soccer Theatre for a meeting of the Church of Constant Crisis.

might those terms be? What's our next move? To shore up our defenses? Is it true that help is on the way is a lie? Is it true that evacuation is really only a sham that has us going to point A to point B to point C to point D to point A? Should we establish a regimen to which we strictly adhere? Have we not much boning up to do before confronting the crisis? Don't we often stand in line and start talking to an Adept or a Shade and then realize we have made fools of ourselves? Do we dream? Can we recall our last dreams? Are these questions going to help us when the crisis comes? What do you make of the Adepts' refusal to join us? Why won't they go away? Can we be more troubled than we are? Are these teeth in our heads real? Is our peduncle, the stalk-like bundle of nerve fibers connecting various parts of our brain, in proper working order? That paltry surrogate for that which we've never understood, the self, what does it have to do with the crisis? Could thirteen geniuses solve the crisis? Is the crisis due to the fact that even though we're dead we can't find our dead mother? Will crawling into a lean-to help? Has someone already anticipated us? Are all the lean-tos occupied? When was the last time we looked into a mirror? Is the crisis to come or is it already here? Is it to come? Already here?

At which point the crowd begins to sway, to murmur, then flail madly about, as the preacher shifts from the interrogative mode to the more fragmented incoherence of the second part of the service, which is called "Going On After It's Over":

Going on. Not going on. This no light, this pall. Despair. Stupidity. That's good. The tongue is an envelope and

99

when sealed there's no end to this. Begin again against the wall. Come into my arms. We can't kid them for long. Little headless figures in the swarm of the eye. The bending of a thumbnail. Remember that. Kneecaps as big as balloons. A blood clot dangling from the nose. Instant eradication. Toss the matches in the pool, sink our toes into the flames. Hold it. Now see here how our endocranial trousers respond to the new wet. Well. Very well. What takes away the shadow? Sinking, floating; floating, sinking. A chiasmus! Language into the vat. Scrabbling in the dust. The dust-coated tongues. One thing and then the next thing. What else! We can't go on a trip dressed like this. Is this the place? This is the only place. The place for what? Everyone is welcome. Pick up your trousers. Stand at attention. Tiny holes in the air. Good. Go on. Don't go on. Right in the middle. The whole sinister saga. The backdrops. Nothing else. Summoning a last. A last flutter. A last last. Very good. Too bad about the weather. Don't say a word. Nailed frowns! Maledictions. Fastigium! That's it. Flail, flail. You can't bleed. All for the best. Yes yes. Always. It'll never stop. The white of the eyes to bursting . . .

And now the congregation is wailing so loudly they drown out the preacher, who leaps into the chaos at his feet and is swept along with the crowd back into the street where for some time they continue their wailing and flailing about.

This service seems to provide its members only a brief relief from anxiety, for a few hours later they reassemble to await another.

Two Theoretical Concerns

IN EACH EDITION OF *THE LITTLE BOOK* I LIKE TO include a few tidbits for the more ambitious reader. Here are two essays you may find challenging.

No writer has sufficiently explained the first phenomenon discussed here,[1] but it is one that will provoke a delight you may have missed in your sublunary life. The following is excerpted

---

[1] See, however, attempts by Silas Haslam, *The Hare of the Tortoise*; Ezra Buckley, *A Rift in the Feathers*; Herbert Ashe, *The Abyss That Embraces*; Jacques Reboul, *The Seeker Sought*; Letizia Alvarez de Toledo, *Racing Alice*; Rudolf v. B. Rucker, *Infinity Is Mine*; et al.

from L. J. Osberg's 1899 *The Race* (which appeared in the Appendix to the 11th edition of *The Little Book*):

THE BEMUSED TORTOISE, THE BEWILDERED HARE

First, a basic description of one of Zeno's paradoxes, more or less in Zeno's words, may be in order:

> If there is space, it will be in something; for all that is is in something, and to be in something is to be in space. This goes on ad infinitum, therefore there is no space.

> Achilles must first reach the place from which the tortoise started. By that time the tortoise will have got on a little way. Achilles must then traverse that, and still the tortoise will be ahead. Achilles is always coming nearer, but he never makes up to it.

> The third argument against the possibility of motion through a space made up of points is that, on this hypothesis, an arrow in any given moment of its flight must be at rest in some particular point.

Crude, yes, but as Wittgenstein wrote (in a somewhat different context), "A point in space is a place for an argument."[2]

---

[2] For a further elucidation of Zeno's paradoxes, see J. L. Borges's chapter on the Tortoise in his *Biography of the Infinite*.

Our purpose, however, is not to argue with the learned scholars of the past or to discuss the abyss Zeno of Elea opened in the landscape of common sense. We simply want to alert you to the seemingly fantastic scene you will no doubt soon encounter, in order that you won't question your so-called sanity or think you are hallucinating or dreaming.

Perhaps you will turn a corner and see at the end of the street, where the landscape opens out to a flat terrain, a crowd gathering to no purpose you can understand, so you approach to investigate. Or perhaps you will have seen, pasted to a wall or pole or lean-to, an advertisement for a race, rather THE RACE:

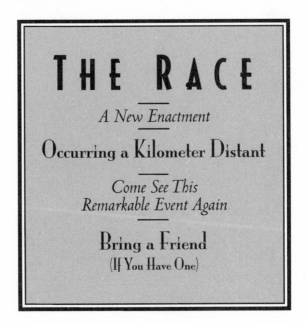

THE RACE

A New Enactment

Occurring a Kilometer Distant

Come See This
Remarkable Event Again

Bring a Friend
(If You Have One)

Regardless of how you come upon the scene, you will find always a young man or woman, trim, athletic, in running shorts and shoes, and beside her (let's say the runner is female this time) will be a tortoise, shelled and sleepy. "On your mark," you will hear the starter say, "get set, GO!" and off they'll go . . . or will they?

What is it you are seeing? Is this a race or a painting? A dream? A film?

The runner is fleet, she moves swiftly across the landscape. The tortoise is slow, barely moving from one point to the next. But . . . the runner never appears to pass the tortoise. Dust puffs up behind the runner's feet, she churns out the yards; the tortoise bobs its slow head toward the ground, lifts its right foreleg, sets it down, lifts its left back leg, sets it down, lifts its left foreleg, sets it down, lifts etc., but so slowly does the tortoise move, just watching it makes you yawn.

So you look back at the runner who is desperately trying to catch up to the tortoise. She races on, but a vast distance separates her from the finish line. And yet she covers the ground enviously fast.

You don't understand. What is going on here? Some in the crowd ooh and ahh, others take notes, still others are photographing the event.

Eventually, the runner tires, gives up, bewildered. The tortoise, who also has yet to achieve the finish line, appears bemused, then strolls off the track.

The crowd disperses.

You look around for an explanation, but none is forthcoming. This scene and its variations (a hare may be substituted for the runner, or you may encounter an archer and the target his speeding arrow can never reach) you are sure to come upon again and again in the Afterlife.

The following theoretical note was delivered at a conference in 1989 by Rotnac and Rekcur and is presented here as one of the numerous attempts to comprehend the physics of the Afterlife.

ANTIMATTER

As conceived by Zöllner, Sarfatti, Feynman, et al., the argument goes like this: Every (generic) particle has, as we know, its counterpart, a corresponding antiparticle. For the negatively charged electron, for example, it's the positron. For the charmed quark, it's the charmed antiquark.[3] Posit then, if you will, a universe that mirrors this universe, a universe where matter is reversed, an antiuniverse. But just as a mirror is not an exact duplication of what it reflects (three dimensions become two, left becomes right, etc.), the antiuniverse is not an exact replication of the (positive) universe.

Do you see where we're going with this? Yes, it is possible the Afterlife, these theorists believe, is a "mirror image" of the (previous) universe, that the Afterlife is an antiuniverse.

[3] It might be apposite here to recall that the mating of a charmed quark with a charmed antiquark would not outwardly display charm because the antiquark would cancel the charm of the quark.

Now, let's take it a step further. Consider again the antielectron, the positron. On earth, the positrons created in particle accelerators have a brief shelf life because inevitably they will come into contact with an electron that will annihilate them. We also know that every time a positron is created, so is an electron, but there are many more detectable electrons on earth than there are detectable positrons. Is it that at "pair production" (the formation of the positron A instigating electron B, which has its own travel line), before the positron meets its counterpart (electron C) and they mutually annihilate one another, the "trace" electron (A) does not in its turn generate (dialectically, if you will) a partner positron? Or is it that there exists somewhere in "space" or "hyperspace" a region where positrons dominate? And is this region then not the Afterlife?

If the answer is yes, then this theory goes a long way in explaining much of the phenomena we encounter here and even the concepts of death and afterdeath. Consider: our terrestrial bodies contained a wealth of electrons, but only a few positrons. At death, in a manner analogous to pair production, this was reversed and we were shuttled along the travel lines of these positrons to where we are now. It's possible to conceive the stages of crossing over as that journey of the body trace along the travel line of the positrons before they contact the travel line of the oncoming electrons and the two sets annihilate themselves, leaving behind a trace of a trace, i.e., us, and the ensuing radiation, i.e., the medium of the Afterlife.[4]

[4] One problem with this notion is that no one has detected any radiation in the Afterlife.

In Feynman's original (i.e., terrestrial) configuration, the particles were one particle, with the two electrons (C and B) moving forward in time and the positron (A) moving backward. If this were true, then we who inhabit the positronic Afterlife should also be moving backward. But, as you know, we don't. We are not "antimen abiding antlike in an antiland" (in Alfau's adept phrasing), but that which we are, inhabitants of the Afterlife, i.e., the dead.

Rudolf v. B. Rucker (*Infinity Can Be Yours*) takes the concept of antimatter to its proper end when he says that not only is this "universe" one of antimatter where "antiatoms consisting of positrons orbit around an antinucleus of antineutrons and antiprotons, but that within that nucleus is a universe where antiantiatoms consisting of antipositrons orbit around an antiantinucleus of antiantineutrons and antiantiprotons, and within that nucleus is a universe where antiantiantiatoms consisting of antiantipositrons orbit around an antiantiantinucleus of antiantiantineutrons and antiantiantiprotons, and within that nucleus is a universe where antiantiantiantiatoms consisting of antiantiantipositrons orbit around an antiantiantiantinucleus of antiantiantiantineutrons and antiantiantiantiprotons, *und so weiter.*"

FURTHER (AND HIGHLY RECOMMENDED) READING

EARTHLY BIBLIOGRAPHERS CAN BE RELIED ON to answer at least three questions about every work they list: Who published it, where, and when? In the Afterlife the first of these is never answered, because it's taken for granted that the author published it, the second is never answered because the best one can do with anyone's location in the Afterlife is to describe it in vague and relative terms, and the third is seldom answered—beyond perhaps noting a decade or a century—because few books are dated (it's considered a bit pretentious).

GENERAL WORKS OF GUIDANCE

New arrivals in the Afterlife want immediate answers to all their questions, which vary little from individual to individual: Where am I? What is my body made of? What's going to happen to me? What is the nature of the beings I see around me? How can I find my friends and relatives? And so on. It is the function of *The Little Book* to provide these answers. I have been asked: Since conditions in the Afterlife are invariable, why do you put out a new edition of *The Little Book* every few years? The answer is twofold. First, while the Afterlife is invariable, the experience that people have of it is not; a few hundred years ago, people expected to see Heaven, Hell, or Purgatory in the Afterlife—and they generally did (much to their initial confusion). Obviously if *The Little Book* had been in print in the fifteenth century, it would have been vastly different from the present volume. Readers of each generation are reassured when they see contemporary references and language in *The Little Book;* it makes them feel they're getting "the true gen." Second, the preparation of successive editions of *The Little Book* is my occupation; it is, as we say, "what keeps me alive."

Since publishing is not pursued for monetary gain in the Afterlife, similar books are seldom written for the same "market." Thus *The Little Book* has no competitors and is without doubt the most widely read book in the Afterlife. It is, in fact, the only book that is "issued" by the habitat itself. As explained in Chapter Four, people generally receive a copy by one means or another within minutes of arrival, when their distress is registered by their surrounding environment. It circulates in English and all other Indo-European languages. Modified versions appear in most Afro-Asiatic (or Hamito-Semitic) tongues. No similar publications exist in the languages of sub-Saharan Africa, Southeast Asia, or Oceania, the information needs of arrivals from these areas being met in a multitude of other ways, such as the "thought pellets" of China, the "waves of knowing" of Oceania, and the enchanting "Three Mooncrane Song" of Japan.

Once immediate anxieties have been laid to rest, newcomers begin to cast about for a direction for the future and naturally seek guidance from books. A perennial favorite for several decades has been *So Now You're Dead!* by the prolific Scots writer Margaret Oliphant (1828–97); this is a light-hearted but level-headed look at "starting over" in the Afterlife, with particular attention given to breaking unfruitful behavior patterns acquired in life.

Take My Advice, edited by John Bartlett (compiler of the famed *Familiar Quotations*), assembles useful accounts of "getting started again" by the likes of Gustav Mahler, Charles Lewis Tiffany, David Belasco, Clarence Darrow, and Calvin Coolidge; as this list suggests, the book could use a bit of updating, but its contents have inspired millions and will continue to do so for generations to come.

Diogenes' Bowl,[1] by an unknown author, dates from the seven-

---

[1] The Diogenes of the title, the same one who took a lantern into the daylit streets of Athens to search for a good man, was said to live in a borrowed tub; so great was his disdain for wealth that when he saw a boy drink from his cupped hands, he discarded his sole possession, his bowl.

teenth century but has never been surpassed as a guide to what can be accomplished by self-discipline and self-organization in the Afterlife beginning (as we all do) with empty hands.

THE AFTERLIFE IN GENERAL

***What** We Know and Don't Know About the Afterlife,* by Isaac Asimov (in life, I'm told, "a distinguished and prolific science writer") is one of the most remarkable and readable volumes ever produced on the subject—and is made all the more remarkable by the fact that the author, as of this writing, has been in our midst for not much more than a year. A banquet for the intellectually curious, this book is precisely the inventory promised in the title.

Mechanisms of the Afterlife, by Georg von Hertling (1843–1919), a German statesman and philosopher, is, as its title suggests, a review of the way things work in the Afterlife, from the stages of decay of a Husk to the replenishment of goods in a store, including many obscure and seldom-noticed processes. A trifle heavy-handed in the Teutonic manner but well observed and admirably detailed.

Butterflies in the Afterlife, by Lillian Nordica (1859–1914), the American soprano once noted for her Marguerite in *Faust,* compiled this dubious catalogue of 1001 Afterlife lepidoptera, amongst which one finds the Singing Butterfly *(Sopranus plexippus),* the Donkey Butterfly *(Asinus rapae),* and an assortment of other fantastical insects. When questioned about their authenticity, Ms. Nordica has stated variously that she studied entomology at Harvard "with the best of them," that she has specimens of each

111

butterfly catalogued and will show it to you if you can tell her how to get to the "other side of the other side," and, more cryptically, that "the butterfly forgot to wake up."

Louise Davis (1924–76), a fifth grade teacher for twenty years in Lake Charles, Louisiana, who, during her life, claimed to have been visited by her dead father and several aunts, wrote over eight hundred letters (these letters are on file at the Central Registry, but have little historical or aesthetic value) to these relatives once she crossed over, but received not a single reply. Her *What Death Is Not*, a remarkable tour de force, at times brilliant, at other times stunningly dull,[2] consists entirely of sentences in the negative: "Death is not the self shining through the body like a flashlight through a window. Death is not the super-physical self robed in a glorious vesture of amethyst, ammonia, and gold. Death is not a song. Death is not the cold blue silence of interstellar space. Death is not the full weight of the downward condition of unliberation and the propensities for standing too long before the wheel of ignorance. Death is not a slow boat to China. Death is not an empty glove. [Et cetera.]" A public reading from the work, mistaken for a pious exercise, is said to have been the founding inspiration for the religion of the Nay-Sayers.

Newcomers startled by their first encounter with a phantasm are further startled to learn that almost nothing has been published on the subject. Writing a book about phantasms is rather like writing a book about large cakes or strangely shaped toes.

---

[2] And somewhat reminiscent of *Jubilate equus onager*, the Afterlife masterpiece of Christopher Smart (1722–71).

Why would one bother? Nonetheless, if you are avid for such reading, look for *Phantasms I Have Known,* by Arthur Godfrey (1903–83), a popular American entertainer of the 1950s. He chronicles his encounters with "the web-footed house," "the grizzled gray tree roo who wore a hat," "the formless hand," "the frog prince," "the sunbonnet of Lucerne," "the cordless telephone," "the ukelele mountain," "the glypdodon who loved a mouse," "the upright donkey," "the fur-lined Edsel," and other equally innocuous and boring emanations. Evidently Mr. Godfrey thought this work would be a great hit in the Afterlife, and copies exist in abundance.

Vladimir Nabokov (1899–1977), the Russian-American scientist and author of *Lolita, Pale Fire, Invitation to a Beheading,* and *The Gift,* was, in life, deeply interested in the Afterlife and the means by which one could cross over. (The main thrust of his approach to crossing over was, I'm told, a potent blend of aesthetics and ethics.) To date, Mr. Nabokov has written only a single work, *The Mysterious Mental Maneuver,* which the jacket claims is the definitive Afterlife text regarding the next stage of our passage. The "text" itself, you discover when you open the book, consists of a seemingly infinite number of exceptionally thin, transparent pages. Unlike Mr. Godfrey's volume, examples of *Maneuver* are exceedingly hard to come by.

TRAVEL AND BIOGRAPHY

The Search for Homer's Shade, by archaeologist-adventurer Heinrich Schliemann (1822–90), discoverer of the site of Troy, the city celebrated in Homer's *Iliad*, is a classic of epic proportions, encompassing a fascinating sixty year "journey of detection" in twenty-seven weighty volumes. Complete sets are hard to find; ask round for a Schliemann club. In 1953 Schliemann announced that he was setting out to find the shade of Noah; his present whereabouts are unknown.

Who's Where in the Underworld? has no counterpart in any earthly publishing venture. Volumes (which may be massive tomes or slender pamphlets) are not organized alphabetically, temporally, or geographically, and may be added to the series by anyone at any time. If you have a burning desire to interview the Roman emperor Nero, consult volume XXVI, which will give you directions that worked for someone writing in the second decade of the nineteenth century. Unfortunately, there is no central publisher in charge of numbering the volumes, so there are at least six volumes numbered XXVI; all the same, one of those six will tell you where Nero was to be found a century and a half ago. Who knows? He may still be there.

Travels Through the Afterlife, by William Habington (1605–54), the poet who memorialized his wife, Lucy, in a cycle of love poems on the theme of chastity and author of the play *The Queen of Aragon*, is one of the most curious volumes in the Afterlife, consisting primarily of the phrase "weeping like a pretty Japanese girl" maddeningly repeated throughout the book's 598 pages, as in the following from page 452: "In order not to weep like a pretty Japanese girl, I travelled in early September to the Bavarian Alps where I saw many beautiful cows, none of them weeping like a pretty Japanese girl, then I returned to the road and, in order not to weep like a pretty Japanese girl, travelled to Berlin, where I stayed for four days and visited the British Book Shop where the clerks were drinking PG Tips but also where no one was weeping like a pretty Japanese girl, then to the Berlin Zoo where it was raining hard enough to make one weep like a pretty Japanese girl, and then to Innsbruck where I took walks through the mountains, none of which were weeping like a pretty Japanese girl, then caught a bad cold, felt very much like weeping like a pretty Japanese girl or leaping out the window, then dreamed I saw Lucy dressed in a kimono, which pleased me almost enough to weep like a pretty Japanese girl, but alas it was only a dream, so I walked down the road until I came to the city of Zurich where I was sure to see, or so I thought, pretty girls or women of French, German, Italian, and, who knows, perhaps even Japanese descent, but there I saw no one, so that I wanted to weep like a pretty Japanese girl but composed myself and stumbled on toward the approaching ash cloud . . ." Never once in the travelogue does Habington encounter a young or old woman or even a child of Oriental descent.

The Seven, by Lucy Terry (1730–1821), the first African-American poet, is the record of her search for the six men and one woman ambushed in a Vermont meadow by Indians on August 25, 1746, whom she wrote about in her poem "Bars Fight." Ms. Terry's interviews with the participants in the battle, none of whom knew they had been immortalized in verse, is a fascinating record of the problems colonial Americans had adjusting to the habitat. The only member of the Seven she has yet to locate is Eunice Allen ("And had not her petticoats stopped her, / The awful creatures had not catched her, / Nor tommy hawked her on the head, / And left her on the ground for dead"), but Ms. Terry confidently states, "She's here somewhere, I know it, and I'll find her if it's the last thing I do."

RELIGION AND MYTHOLOGY

Myths and Legends of the Hereafter, collected in fifty-six volumes by the renowned Danish theologian, mythologist, and poet Nikolai Grundtvig (1783–1872), is one of the marvels of the Afterlife, a labor requiring more than a century to complete. It's said that, when he realized that it *was* at last complete, Grundtvig threw himself from a precipice (but of course failed of the desired object of ending his existence).

Upon arrival in the Afterlife, Philip Melanchthon (1497–1560), the overly conciliatory successor to Martin Luther, immediately shed his Greek name for his original German one, Schwarzerd, and founded his own (nominal) religion, Black Earth. His *Black Earth Credo,* a work of great power and obscurity, seems to discover the source of the habitat's efficacy in the remains of Husks. If there were blood to be shed among the dead, it would have been shed over this strange and difficult work, which is rediscovered, reinterpreted, and battled over anew every twenty years or so.

THE ARTS

Delia Salter Bacon (1811–59) died obsessed with the notion that "the divine William [Shakespeare] is the biggest and most successful fraud ever practiced on a patient world"[3] and arrived in the Afterlife still obsessed with it. Having failed in life to open Shakespeare's tomb to obtain proof that the plays were written by a consortium led by Francis Bacon (no relation, though in her later years she began to imagine that he was one) and including Sir Walter Raleigh, Edmund Spenser, Sir Philip Sidney, and others, she succeeded in tracking down the shade of the Bard of Avon and began to badger him for a "confession." After a few years, Shakespeare invoked an enfolding of Adepts, which was maintained for a decade or so, until Miss Bacon finally agreed that "the matter doesn't amount to a hill of beans." She tells her story with surprising good humor in *Time's Glory.*[4]

Wovoka (1856?–1932), a Paiute Indian prophet of the Ghost Dance, whose "bulletproof ghost shirt," decorated with stars, birds, and arrows proved inefficacious to the Indians massacred at Wounded Knee, wrote *The Tale of the Shirt,* an allegorical tragedy in the form of a children's story, about a prideful shirt in search of a "good body" to protect, but it turns out that in the country where the shirt lives, there are no human beings. When you encounter a mournful shade endlessly chanting "Wovoka, Wovoka" as he trudges down the road, you can be reasonably sure this is a reader of that story.

---

[3] A reader of the 48th Edition of *The Little Book* tells me that, though these words exactly describe Miss Bacon's belief, they must be attributed to Henry James, whose uncle is said to have been a friend of hers. My informant on this point is, however, unable to tell me whether they should be attributed to the novelist or to his father, the American philosopher of the same name.

[4] From a line in Shakespeare's *The Rape of Lucrece:* "Time's glory is to calm contending kings, to unmask falsehood, and bring truth to light."

Gedichte Auch (Poems, Too), the "sunniest" sonnet cycle you're ever likely to read, is even more remarkable when you consider that the author is Georg Trakl (1887–1914), the Austrian expressionist, who during his terrestrial existence reveled in despair and decay. On this side, however, one frequently sees him frolicking hand in hand with young women. Also of interest is his charming comedy in verse, *The Man Who Knew His Sister.*

PERSONAL HISTORY

Revenge isn't an emotion that lasts long in the Afterlife; those who wronged you in life are not so much forgiven as quickly forgotten, or seen simply as irrelevant. This has not been the case, however, for Yang Kuei-fei (719–756), the concubine of the T'ang emperor Hsüan Tsung and the most famous beauty in Chinese history, who was executed by the emperor at the insistence of his disgruntled soldiers. Her *My Death in Life, My Life in Death*, is, among other things, a remarkably impassioned plea for the rights of women and at the same time a truly warped diatribe against her own people. In the latest edition of her autobiography (she revises it every century), she acknowledges for the first time that Hsüan Tsung has made many attempts to meet her; though he was heartbroken after the deed and soon abdicated his throne, she refuses to see him, stating that his sorrow "holds no truck with me."

The unfortunate postmortem existence of Georges Méliès (1861–1938), the innovative turn-of-the-century filmmaker, is chronicled in his *Let Me Be*, wherein he claims that someone named Rosencrans is controlling his mind and sending him on

118

voyages to war-torn areas of the moon, where he is required to invent fantastic machines to help one side or the other, the inhabitants of *Maro Humorum,* say, or of *Lacus Somniorum.* Further he would have us believe that this Rosencrans is not a resident of the Afterlife but one of the undead still on earth, a young man, he states, who lives in a central Missouri commune that makes peanut butter. That such an occurrence is without precedent (and likelihood) in the Afterlife does not for a moment lessen the anguish we sense in Méliès's *cri de coeur.*

Tesla's Take on Tachyons by Nikola Tesla (1856–1943), the inventor of (among many credited and uncredited inventions) the Tesla coil and the radio and the designer of the power system at Niagara Falls, attempts (unsuccessfully) to make practical application of the "whales on the horizon" phenomenon. If he could convince others to build his designs, which resemble more than anything else the "metamechanic" sculptures of Jean Tinguely, Tesla believes he could "radically transform the habitat," giving only hints of what this transformation might consist of ("winged particles that will unmask Eternity," "the nightmare of reason will illuminate the day"). My favorite moment in the book occurs when, in the introduction, Tesla recalls his first Afterlife meeting with his former employer, Thomas Alva Edison (1847–1931), who had treated him shabbily and taken credit for some of his work. Edison, Tesla relates, had been looking for Tesla for decades to apologize to him for his behavior. They spent a pleasant year together studying the "whale" phenomenon, but Tesla finally concluded that Edison's notions were "childish at best." He leaves us with the image of Edison working enthusiastically on a miniature version of his Kinetoscope.

A small book appeared in London in 1810, when I was

eighteen years old, that prompted me to devote my life to publishing. This book was *Illustrations of Madness*, by John Haslam, who was at that time the chief administrator at Bethlem Hospital, the lunatic asylum popularly known as Bedlam. The book had a single purpose, to explain why one inmate, James Tilly Matthews, was being detained over his family's objections, and it achieved that purpose by setting out in luxuriant detail the fullness of Matthews's bizarre delusions—as described by Matthews himself. Reading this book was an electrifying experience for me and I daresay for thousands of others, for never before (so far as I knew then or know now) had the actual inner workings of madness been set out in this way—not as conjectured by outside observers but as reported and explained (and indeed even skillfully illustrated) by the madman himself.

According to Matthews, his disorders were not the result of any inherent mental derangement within him but rather of the machinations of "a gang of villains profoundly skilled in Pneumatic Chemistry, who assail him by means of an Air Loom," a large and complex machine that sends out crippling waves and rays from a nearby bunker. The gang, led by *Bill the King*, consists of *Jack the Schoolmaster*, who serves as recorder to the gang, *Sir Archy*, thought to be a woman dressing as a man, *Middle Man*, middle-aged and of middling stature, who manufactures Air Looms for use all over London, *Augusta*, who serves as liaison with other gangs in the area, *Charlotte*, herself a captive member of the gang, kept "nearly naked, and poorly fed," and finally the nameless and perpetually silent *Glove Woman*, so named for her cotton mittens, which she wears "because she has got the itch." The list of catastrophic effects the gang is able to produce with the Air

Loom is a long one, including *Fluid locking,* which constricts the fibers at the root of the tongue so as to impede speech, *Cutting soul from sense,* which dissociates emotions from intellect, *Thigh-talking,* which relocates the sense of hearing to the thigh, *Kiteing,* a particularly distressing assailment by which they contrive "to lift into the brain some particular idea, which floats and undulates in the intellect for hours," *Lobster-cracking,* which constricts the magnetic atmosphere around the victim to produce instant death, *Apoplexy-working with the nutmeg-grater,* which violently forces fluids into the head, *Lengthening the brain,* which distorts one's thoughts like a fun-house mirror, *Thought-making,* used to force into the victim's mind "a train of ideas very different from the real subject of his thoughts," *Laugh-making,* a technique for inducing senseless mirth, *Bomb-bursting,* an electrically produced internal explosion, usually fatal, and many other infamous torments such as *Foot-curving, Knee-nailing, Eye-screwing, Sight-stopping, Vital-tearing,* and so on.

Matthews's own "illustrations of madness" confirmed the grounds for his continued incarceration, but Haslam's triumph was short-lived. Soon after Matthews's death in 1815, another document he had written came to light, an indictment of Haslam's administrative malpractices that apparently bore the hallmark of sanity, and a nephew chose this time to come forward with the claim that Haslam had put Matthews in chains for challenging his authority. Although Haslam twice went to print to defend himself, the Bethlem governors decided to minimize the scandal by dismissing him. Although far from crushed, Haslam never completely recovered from this blow, delivered (as it were) from beyond the grave.

In 1841, after nearly three decades as a London publisher (during which time I never realized my dream of producing a work as sensational as *Illustrations of Madness*), I made my own journey to the Other Side. A few months later, when I "had my head on" at last, I was astonished to receive a visit from James Tilly Matthews himself, who, having somehow learned of my career in publishing, asked for my assistance in a literary project he'd been working on since his arrival in the Afterlife; this was a rebuttal of Haslam's book and a "definitive proof" of the reality of the Air Loom and all its nefarious operations. Curious and without other occupation, I allowed him to lead me to his "home," which proved to be nothing less than Bedlam itself, the habitation of tens of thousands of the world's juiciest lunatics, all projecting their extravagant delusions onto their environment and thereby making them as real as rhubarb.

I examined (through binoculars) the infamous Air Loom, still being operated by the gang of seven, and over the next few days learned what it meant to suffer the humiliations of *gas-plucking* and *pushing up the quicksilver* and *stomach-skinning* and many other torments, but this terrible engine did not account for a tenth part of one percent of all the bizarre machinations at work there. I will not attempt to enrich you with a full appreciation of that place—and need not, as you'll see. Matthews and his many collaborators had assembled a veritable encyclopedia on the workings of Bedlam, hundreds of thousands of pages, tens of thousands of meticulous diagrams and drawings . . . and they wondered how in the empyrean they were to turn them into a book! I assured them that, in order to produce anything recognizable as a book, they had to reduce their mountain of paper to

Bedlam: a quiet moment at dusk. "An hour spent among the inmates of this veridical Wonderland," Lewis Carroll is said to have told a friend, "may persuade you that lunacy is the true ultimate end for which the Almighty shaped our race."

at least a small hill, which task, under my direction, they accomplished during the three years that followed.

Toward the end, Matthews began to clamor for a single presentation copy that he needed for "someone who will be arriving in the Afterlife any day now." I asked who this person was and how Matthews knew of his approaching demise, but he merely shook his head and snapped his fingers angrily (as he usually did when he was agitated). Soon the requisite presentation copy was in hand, and the two of us hurried off down the road. Before long an elderly gentleman came tottering toward us, still beset by the staggers that mark the freshly deceased.

Matthews rushed forward and thrust into the newcomer's hands the very first copy of *The Discovery of Bedlam by Its Own Inhabitants*, bound in what passes in the Afterlife as morocco. Ignoring the other's utter flabbergastation, Matthews turned and graciously introduced him to me. I should have foreseen it. It was Matthews's ancient enemy, John Haslam, who had outlived us both, surviving to the ripe old age of eighty.

The Discovery of Bedlam is still "in print" and is one of my proudest achievements.

A few months after its publication, however, feeling at loose ends, I began to cast about for another project. I found it readily enough and was soon hard at work on the first edition of *The Little Book*. This single enterprise has given me a long and rewarding career—and I heartily wish you its equal.

GLOSSARY

ONLY TERMS HAVING A SPECIAL MEANING IN THE Afterlife are included in this Glossary. For those whose meaning is fundamentally the same as in life (like *club, greeter, horizon, medium,* and so on), consult the Index.

Adept. A member of the second most numerous "human" component of the Afterlife population (after Regulars); Adepts are sweet, tranquil, doll-like beings who speak their own language and keep their own company, exclusively. Many assume they are the never-born or the not-yet-born.

Afterlife religion. A religion having no counterpart or antecedent among the living. See the Index for extensive references to this subject.

Bedlam. A region of uncertain extent populated by the shades of institutionalized lunatics. Although not in any sense institutionalized in the Afterlife, many of these shades (whether actually deranged or not) remain in Bedlam, apparently preferring the company of their own kind.

Blood-draining deities. In the mythology of the Radiant, three very exacting examiners who screen pilgrims at the fifth stage of crossing over and later take possession of those who backslide at the ninth.

Brightness. An infrequent, short-lived aerial phenomenon, cause unknown, resembling "the sun behind clouds" and regarded by some as a divine or angelic manifestation.

Catacombs. Subsurface residences, storage areas, and passages found throughout the Afterlife.

Central Registry. A bureau devoted to the collection of names and locations of the dead.

Crossing religion. A religion founded on the expectation that, individually or collectively, we will someday ascend to a higher plane of being.

The Dark Brother. A mysterious spirit being who, having no corporeal residence of his own in the Afterlife, briefly makes his home in each of us by turns.

Deadhead. A shade who is excessively overwhelmed or fascinated by the fact of his or her death.

Digger. A member of the Guild of Diggers; loosely speaking, any explorer or resident of the catacombs.

Dweller on the Threshold. In the mythology of the Radiant, the guardian of the fourth stage of crossing over. He is considered a neutral sentinel, one who will neither help nor hinder the seeker.

Eidolon. A phantom, often conceived as the "projection" of a living being forward or backward into the future or past.

Eidolonism. A somewhat esoteric theory or belief that the Afterlife is a system of eidolonic projections. To summarize briefly and partially, Husks are (according to this theory) projections "forward" from those who die *in utero* or in infancy to an unrealized adulthood, and Adepts are projections "backward" from the unborn to Platonic Ideals.

Empyrean. The domain of the Afterlife.

Fiery globes. Pulsating red spots that appear aperiodically before the eyes, seemingly just beyond arm's reach.

126

Flame-enhaloed Deities. In the mythology of the Radiant, fiery figures that are attracted to pilgrims who hesitate between steps during the Thirteen Stages of Crossing Over. Some identify them as Fiery Globes.

Four Females Who Keep the Door. In the mythology of the Radiant, deities who have the power to enable the pilgrim to cross over at the end of stage thirteen.

Guild religion. A religion practiced by members of an Afterlife guild.

Guild of the Dark Brother. Probably the largest of the Afterlife guilds, devoted to the cult of the Dark Brother (q.v.).

Have your head on. Become reconciled to death and accustomed to the workings of the Afterlife.

He Who Is Truly Small. An epithet for the Dark Brother, used to avoid a direct reference, which is thought by some to be unlucky.

Hiranyagabha. In the mythology of the Radiant, the monster guardian of the jewel that must be presented to the Four Females Who Keep the Door (q.v.).

Husk. A member of the least numerous "human" component of the Afterlife population (after Regulars and Adepts); Husks are thought to be imperfectly realized "adult" eidolons of those who die *in utero* or in infancy; they are large, unpleasant to be around, and harmless. They eventually disintegrate; the Adepts collect and dispose of the remains.

Karroum. The skinless, not to be confused with their whole-skinned followers, who call themselves the Skinless.

Lokas. Weapons that, according to followers of the Khaki Bodhisattva among the Radiant, are used to inflict pain on the unenlightened during the crossing over.

Lose your head. Suffer death.

Memory-loss hysteria. A brief, localized mass delusion in which all believe that they have been struck "memory-dead."

Never-born. See **Adept.**

Northern Cities. Cities of perpetual "daylight," so-called after the far-north cities of the earth, which, at the height of the summer, experience round-the-clock sunlight.

Phantasm. An ephemeral apparition, generally odd and out of place.

Prana. In Hindu religion the "breath of life," experienced in the Afterlife as a rosy light cascading through our bodies. It is said that in the earthly work *Bengal Lancer,* F. Yeats-Brown wrote: "There was a *saddhi* at Puri who claimed to be able to resurrect sparrows by breathing *prana* into them." In *Yoga,* J. Hewitt wrote: "The power of the atom is Prana. Thought is Prana. . . . It pervades the whole universe."

The Radiant. Members of the Afterlife's most popular crossing religion.

Reconstruction. An earthly text assembled from the memory of the dead.

Regular. A member of the most numerous "human" component of the Afterlife population; it is thought that all who survive infancy become Regulars in the Afterlife.

Reunion. See **Walling-in.**

Shade. A Regular; one of the dead. The term is usually used to avoid confusion between present relationships ("my friend Paul") and those enjoyed in life ("the shade of my friend Paul").

The Six. Six shades, who, according to the beliefs of the Letheans, long ago achieved the state to which they aspire, that of total nirvanic oblivion.

The skinless. The Karroum (q.v.); when capitalized, the word refers to the (whole-skinned) followers of the Karroum.

Society of Fools. A large, variegated guild of entertainers.

Spontaneous (or "Street-Corner") religion. A religion that appears or is practiced on the spur of the moment.

The Staggers. The tremulous gait characteristic of the very recently deceased.

Store. An accumulation of goods free for the taking.

Tachyon. A particle that travels faster than light.

Walling-in. A ritual occasionally practiced by catacomb-dwellers. The candidate is walled into a tight-fitting niche (an act deliberately mimetic of the soul's former imprisonment in the body) in hopes of achieving an ecstatic transformation known as Reunion.

INDEX

134

The Road . . . an endless invitation to wonders beyond enumeration. Here a dusty pilgrim approaches the Valley of Stelae, a region of monuments so ancient that their origins are literally lost in time.